STUDIA
TURCOLOGICA
CRACOVIENSIA

11

Jagiellonian University · Institute of Oriental Philolology

Studia
Turcologica
Cracoviensia

11

Edited by
Stanisław Stachowski

Kraków 2008

JAGIELLONIAN UNIVERSITY · INSTITUTE OF ORIENTAL PHILOLOLOGY

KAMIL STACHOWSKI

NAMES OF CEREALS
IN THE TURKIC LANGUAGES

KRAKÓW 2008

Reviewer
Henryk Jankowski

Proofreading
Kinga Maciuszak

Cover design
Kamil Stachowski

This volume has appeared
thanks to the financial support
of the Jagiellonian University's
Faculty of Philology

ISBN 978-83-7188-098-8

Księgarnia Akademicka
ul. św. Anny 6, 31–008 Kraków
tel./fax: (012) 431·27·43
tel.: 422·10·33 wew. 11·67
akademicka@akademicka.pl
www.akademicka.pl

CONTENTS

AIM AND SCOPE OF THIS WORK

The aim of this work is to work out the etymologies of the names of the seven most important cereals (**barley** *Hordeum* L., **corn** *Zea mays* L., **millet** *Panicum* L., **oats** *Avena* L., **rice** *Oryza Sativa* L., **rye** *Secale Cereale* L., and **wheat** *Triticum* L.) in the Turkic languages.

The current, rather uneven state of comparative dialectology and lexicography of the Turkic languages does not allow us to perform full comparisons. We have therefore limited ourselves to literary names, and only included selected dialectal forms. For the same reason, the names of subspecies and varieties have been excluded.

STATE OF ART AND SOURCES

Our subject has not as yet been dealt with as a whole. Of the papers in the Turkic languages that are devoted to the names of plants (not just cereals) the most detailed has been written L.V. Dmitrieva (1972). This, however, only contains an extremely limited commentary. Etymological propositions for various names in single languages are scattered in etymological dictionaries, generally only accompanied by a brief explanation, and in numerous articles where a more comprehensive commentary is usually provided.

The bulk of the sources used in this paper are dictionaries, mainly Russian post-revolutionary ones (abbreviated RKirgS, TuwRS &c.), also etymological dictionaries (an especially large amount of data is to be found in ÈSTJa), various articles and publications devoted to the vocabulary and/or grammar of single languages, and descriptions of dialects (mainly Turkish).

STRUCTURE OF AN ENTRY

– Alphabetical list of forms ordered by pronunciation
  Enables a preliminary investigation of the phonetical diversity of names. All variants are ordered alphabetically and linked with a system of cross-references.
– Alphabetical list of forms ordered by languages
  Presents the diversity of the names in one language. Comparing the stock of names in languages from one group can help to find out which forms should be treated as the standard ones.
– Brief overview of previous etymologies
  For lesser investigated words, we have tried to summarise the entire literature available to us. For those which are better known, we have only selected the most important works. All papers have been treated equally, including the ones which we cannot be ready to accept, given the present state of art.
– Commentary
  The commentary consists of a discussion with the propositions summarised before and a presentation of our own views.

TRANSCRIPTION

We have tried to present all Turkic forms in a unified, phonological transcription. The distinction between palatal *k*, *g* : velar *q*, *γ* has only been preserved for OUyg., Uyg. and Uzb., as in all the other languages it is unequivocally determined by the position. By the same token, we have abandoned the marking of labialization of *a* in Uzb. (as resulting systematically from the orthography) and of spirantization of *s* and *z* in Trkm.; however, we have preserved it in Bšk. where it has a phonological significance. Apart from this, a dual transcription has been employed for *e*: wide *ä* vs narrow *e* for languages where they are separate phonemes, and neutral *e* for the others.

THANKS

I am grateful to many people for helping me in various ways. Most of all, I would like to express my special gratitude to (alphabetically):
- Professor Árpád Berta (Szeged, Hungary) for expert advice and access to his working materials,
- László Károly, MA (Szeged, Hungary) for helping me access some of the more inaccessible literature,
- Doctor Kinga Maciuszak (Cracow, Poland) for professional advice and Iranistic help,
- Professor Andrzej Pisowicz (Cracow, Poland) for professional advice and Iranistic help,
- Professor Marek Stachowski (Cracow, Poland) for a great amount of help and time without which this work would not be completed,
- Professor Alexander Vovin (Honolulu, USA) for Sinological help.

BARLEY
HORDEUM L.

Barley was one of the first domesticated cereals in the world. The oldest grains of spelt are thought to be nine thousand years old, and have been found in Jarmo, Kurdistan from where it probably originates. Its cultivation had spread westwards from this region around the 5th millennium BC, to Mespotamia, Egypt and elsewhere.

Domesticated barley (*Hordeum vulgare*) is believed to have originated from the eastern part of the Central Asian Centre, from where it spread West and South-West, i.e. to India, Persia, Mesopotamia, Syria and Egypt, and later to Greece and Italy (4th c. BC) and even further.

The area between Siberia and the Pacific is now used for the cultivation of barley, but the plant was only introduced there in the 19th c.

Compared to other cereals, especially to wheat which is equally old, or perhaps even older, barley has very few varieties: 29 species, including 16 stable, but they already existed in the second half of the 4th millennium BC. In the ancient world, barley was very popular; almost every higher culture cultivated it.

Names for 'barley' are most uniform in the Turkic languages. Almost all languages have the word *arpa*, and all the other names only have a very limited range. Interestingly, barley is quite often identified or confused with oats, and while Tel. *sula* 'barley' < 'oats', all the other examples of this confusion display just the opposite direction of development. This is understandable given the chronology of domestication of these two cereals – cf. commentary on *julaf* (point 2), and *arpakan* and *harva* 'oats', and footnote 1.

FORMS:

apa → arpa	as	ńesemen → žehimien
arba → arpa	aš → as	orpa → arpa
arbaj → arpa	erpe → arpa	sula
arpa	harva → arpa	ša'īr
arpä → arpa	jačmeń	tak-tak
arpagan	köče	urpa → arpa
arpagān → arpagan	köže → köče	žesemen → žehimien
arpakan › arpagan	nečimien → žehimien	žeh
arva → arpa	nehimien → žehimien	žehimien → žehimien
arvaj → arpa	ńečimien → žehimien	žesemen → žehimien

LANGUAGES:

Az.: *arpa*	Com.: *arpa*	Čuv.: *orpa, urpa*
Blk.: *arpa*	Crm.: *arpa*	Gag.: *arpa*
Brb.: *aš*	CTat.: *arpa*	Kar.: *arpa*
Bšk.: *arpa*	Čag.: *arpa*	KarC: *arpa*

KarH: *arpa*
KarT: *arpa*
Khak.: *arba, as, köče*
Khal.: *arpa*
Kirg.: *arpa, arpakan*
Kklp.: *arpa*
Kmk.: *arpa*
Krč.Blk.: *arpa*
Küär.: *arba*
Kyzyl: *arba*
Kzk.: *arpa, tak-tak*
MTkc.: *arpa*
MTkc.H: *arpa*
MTkc.IM: *arpa*

MTkc.KD: *arpa*
MTkc.MA: *arba, arpa*
MTkc.MA.B: *arpä*
MTkc.MK: *arba, arpa,
    arpagān*
Nog.: *arpa*
Oghuz.Ir.: *arpa*
OTkc.: *arpa, arpagan*
Ott.: *arpa, ša'īr*
OUyg.: *arpa*
Oyr.: *arba*
Sag.: *arba*
SarUyg.: *arva, harva*
Šr.: *aš*

Tat.: *arpa, arpagan*
Tat.Gr.: *arpa*
Tel.: *arba, sula*
Tksh.: *arpa*
Tksh.dial.: *žeh*
Tof.: *jačmeń*
Trkm.: *arpa, arpagan*
Tuv.: *arbaj, arvaj, köže*
Uyg.: *apa, arpa, erpe*
Uzb.: *arpa*
Yak.: *nečimien, nehimien,
    ńečimien, ńesemen,
    žesemen, žehimien,
    žesemen*

ARPA

FORMS:

apa **Uyg.**: Raquette 1927, ÈSTJa, Dmitrieva 1979

arba **Khak.**: Dmitrieva 1972, ÈSTJa, Dmitrieva 1979, Çevilek 2005 || **Küär.**: R I 335t,
    Räsänen 1949: 236, Joki 1952, Eren 1999 || **Kyzyl**: Joki 1952, 1953 || **MTkc.MK**: Egorov
    1964 || **MTkc.Zam**: Egorov 1964 || **Oyr.**: R I 335t, Räsänen 1949: 236, Joki 1952,
    Egorov 1964, RAltS, VEWT, Dmitrieva 1972, ÈSTJa, Dmitrieva 1979, Eren 1999,
    Çevilek 2005 || **Sag.**: Joki 1952 || **Tel.**: R I 335t, Räsänen 1949: 236, Joki 1952,
    Ryumina-Sırkaşeva/Kuçigaşeva 1995, Eren 1999

arbaj **Tuv.**: RTuwS, Egorov 1964, Tatarincev 2000–, Çevilek 2005

arpa **Az.**: Räsänen 1949: 236, Joki 1952, RAzS, Egorov 1964, Dmitrieva 1972,
    ÈSTJa || **Blk.**: ÈSTJa || **Bšk.**: RBškS, Egorov 1964, Dmitrieva 1972, ÈSTJa, Eren
    1999 || **Crm.**: Joki 1952 || **CTat.**: Zaatovъ 1906, ÈSTJa || **Čag.**: Räsänen 1949: 236, Joki 1952,
    VEWT || **Gag.**: ÈSTJa || **Kar.**: Joki 1952 || **KarC**: KRPS, Levi 1996 || **KarH**: Mard-
    kowicz 1935, KRPS || **KarT**: Kowalski 1929, KRPS || **Khal.**: Doerfer/Tezcan 1980,
    Doerfer 1987 || **Kirg.**: Mašanovъ 1899, RKirgS-Ju44, RKirgS-Ju57, Egorov 1964,
    Dmitrieva 1972, ÈSTJa, Eren 1999 || **Kklp.**: RKklpS-BB, RKklpS-ST, Egorov 1964,
    RKklpS-B, Dmitrieva 1972, ÈSTJa, Eren 1999 || **Kmk.**: Räsänen 1949: 236, Joki 1952,
    RKmkS, Egorov 1964, Dmitrieva 1972, ÈSTJa || **Krč.Blk.**: RKrčBlkS, Dmitrieva
    1972 || **Kzk.**: RKzkS-46, Räsänen 1949: 236, Joki 1952, RKzkS-54, Egorov 1964, Dmitrieva
    1972, ÈSTJa, DFKzk, Eren 1999 || **MTkc.**: Räsänen 1949: 236 || **MTkc.H**: (ارپا) Houtsma
    1894 || **MTkc.IM**: VEWT || **MTkc.KD**: اربه Golden 2000 || **MTkc.MK**: Joki 1952,
    Dankoff/Kelly 1982–85 || **MTkc.Zam**: Egorov 1964, Dmitrieva 1979 || **Nog.**: RNogS,
    Egorov 1964, Dmitrieva 1972, ÈSTJa || **Oghuz.Ir.**: Doerfer/Hesche 1989 || **OTkc.**: Räsänen
    1949: 236, Joki 1952, Dmitrieva 1972 || **Ott.**: (آرپه) Wiesentahl 1895, Räsänen 1949: 236,
    Joki 1952, VEWT || **OUyg.**: Çevilek 2005 || **Tat.**: Voskresenskij 1894, Imanaevъ 1901,
    آرپا Tanievъ 1909, Räsänen 1949: 236, Joki 1952, RTatS-D, Egorov 1964, Dmitrieva

1972, ÈSTJa, RTatS-G || **Tat.Gr.**: Podolsky 1981 || **Tksh.**: Egorov 1964, Dmitrieva 1972, ÈSTJa, Çevilek 2005 || **Trkm.**: Alijiv/Böörijif 1929, Räsänen 1949: 236, RTrkmS, Nikitin/ Kerbabaev 1962, Egorov 1964, Dmitrieva 1972, Eren 1999, Dmitrieva 1979 || **Uyg.**: Raquette 1927, Räsänen 1949: 236, Joki 1952, RUjgS, Egorov 1964, VEWT, ÈSTJa, Dmitrieva 1972, 1979, Jarring 1998: 14, Çevilek 2005 || **Uzb.**: ارپا Nalivkinъ 1895, Lapin 1899, Smolenskij 1912, RUzbS-A, Egorov 1964, RUzbS-Š, Dmitrieva 1972, ÈSTJa

arpä **MTkc.MA.B**: Borovkov 1971: 99

arva **SarUyg.**: Çevilek 2005

arvaj **Tuv.**: ÈSTJa, Dmitrieva 1979

erpe **Uyg.**: Çevilek 2005

harva **SarUyg.**: Çevilek 2005

urpa **Čuv.**: Nikolьskij 1909, RČuvS-D, RČuvS-E, Egorov 1964, VEWT, RČuvS-A, Dmitrieva 1972, 1979, Eren 1999

LANGUAGES:

Az.: *arpa* || **Blk.**: *arpa* || **Bšk.**: *arpa* || **Com.**: *arpa* || **Crm.**: *arpa* || **CTat.**: *arpa* || **Čag.**: *arpa* || **Čuv.**: *orpa, urpa* || **Gag.**: *arpa* || **Kar.**: *arpa* || **KarC**: *arpa* || **KarH**: *arpa* || **KarT**: *arpa* || **Khak.**: *arba* || **Khal.**: *arpa* || **Kirg.**: *arpa* || **Kklp.**: *arpa* || **Kmk.**: *arpa* || **Krč.Blk.**: *arpa* || **Küär.**: *arba* || **Kyzyl**: *arba* || **Kzk.**: *arpa* || **MTkc.**: *arpa* || **MTkc.H**: *arpa* || **MTkc.IM**: *arpa* || **MTkc.KD**: *arpa* || **MTkc.MA**: *arba, arpa* || **MTkc.MA.B**: *arpä* || **MTkc.MK**: *arba, arpa* || **Nog.**: *arpa* || **Oghuz.Ir.**: *arpa* || **OTkc.**: *arpa* || **Ott.**: *arpa* || **OUyg.**: *arpa* || **Oyr.**: *arba* || **Sag.**: *arba* || **Tat.**: *arpa* || **Tat.Gr.**: *arpa* || **Tel.**: *arba* || **Tksh.**: *arpa* || **Trkm.**: *arpa* || **Tuv.**: *arbaj, arvaj* || **Uyg.**: *apa, arpa, erpe* || **Uzb.**: *arpa*

ETYMOLOGY:

1949: Räsänen: 236: limits himself to a comparison with Mo. *arbaj*, Ma. *arfa*, Afgh. *ōrbūšah*, Gr. ὀλφα [sic; cf. KWb 1976 and Steblin-Kamenskij 1982]

1952: Joki: the Altaic forms belong to the same group as Afgh. and Gr., 'but not directly' against uniting PIE *albhi-*, Gr. ἄλφι and Alb. *el'p* [el'bi]

1963: TMEN 445: Tkc. > Mo. (> Sal., Tuv.; Ma.), Hung. et al.
against the possibility of PIE *albhi-* > Ir. *arpa-*, but does not exclude the possibility of IE origin in general

1964: Egorov: limits himself to enumerating forms from various Tkc. languages

1969: VEWT: limits himself to providing bibliography and remarking that Hung. *árpa* 'barley' < Čuv. *urpa*

1972: Clauson: ? < IE (? Toch.) (referring to TMEN 445)

1974: ÈSTJa: limits himself to summarizing previous propositions

1976: KWb: puts together Tkc. *arpaj* and Ma. *arfa*, Afgh. *ōrbūšah*, Gr. ἄλφι

1979: Dmitrieva 164f.: < OIr. or old IE; or common in Alt. and IE
MTkc.MA *arbaj*, Tuv. *arvaj* < Mo.

1982: Steblin-Kamenskij: puts together Afgh. *orbəši, urbáši* et al. < ? *arpasyā-* (after EVP) and maybe Gr. ἄλφι, ἄλφιτον '(pearl) barley (porridge); flour'

1990: Róna-Tas: 31: quotes the comparison with Gr. *alfiton*, Alb. *el'p* and Ir. *arb/pa* allowing the possibility of < Ir. *arb/pa*, but remarks that the Ir. form has only been reconstructed basing on the Tkc. ones; Ma. *arfa*, Mo. *arbaj* < Tkc.

1993:   EWU: probably from some IE language
Hung. *árpa* 'barley' from some Tkc. language, cf. Uyg., Com. *arpa*, Čuv. *urpa*, *orpa* &c.

1998:   Jarring: 14: probably < IE (? Toch.)

1999:   Eren: limits himself to summarizing previous propositions

2000:   Tatarincev: *ar- 'to multiply oneself, to be numerous' + -p intens. + -a
Joki's 1952 proposition not grounded sufficiently

2000:   Tietze: limits himself to quoting Doerfer's 1993: 85 opinion on borrowing from Mo. to Tkc.

2003:   NEVP: unclear expression: 'if Pashto *orbəša* et al. < *arpasyā*, then cf. Tkc. *arpa*'

2005:   Çevilek: accepts Clauson's 1972 proposition

COMMENTARY:

This word is unusually common in the Tkc. languages, and, at first glance, the phonetic diversity of all its forms is surprisingly small.[1] This commonality might be understood as a sign that the Tkc. people became acquainted with barley very early on, perhaps as one of the first cereals. The uniformity of the sounding should probably be attributed to the phonetically very simple structure of the word, which does not provoke any serious changes by itself.[2] The meaning of the word is the same everywhere, too, except for 1. SarUyg. *harva* which means both 'barley' and 'oats' (cf.), 2. for an obvious influence of Russ. in Bšk., Tat. and Tksh. meanings of 'stye' (after ÈSTJa; see also VEWT), and 3. for a simple semantic shift in Az.dial. 'ladies' barley grain shaped decoration' &c. (after ÈSTJa).

The name is also present in the Mo. and Ma. languages, where it is probably a loanword from Tkc. cf. ÈSTJa for further bibliography.

Almost all the etymologists dealing with this word limit themselves to quoting previous works (often quite inaccurately) about the possible Ir. origin.[3] Only some of them add their own commentary, which is usually not particularly innovative.

---

1   Perhaps Sal. *arfa* and Tuv. *arva* deserve a bit more interest, as the spirantization of *p* could be regarded as a trace that these forms are not a continuation of OTkc. *arpa*, but rather borrowings from one of the Mo. languages (cf. Klmk.dial. *arva* – however, meaning 'oats'), or alternately, though this does not seem very probable due to cultural-historical reasons, from Ma. *arfa* 'oats; barley' (cf. *julaf* 'oats'). However, it might be equally probable that the spirantization is a trivial innovation in these languages, cf. SarUyg. *harva* 'oats'.
Also Sal. *ahrun* 'barley flour' < *arfa un* (Kakuk 1962: 175) has a strange sounding which does not seem to be explicable by any regular phonetic law.

2   However, beyond the Tkc. languages the situation is not so simple any more. A Ma. form *arfa* quoted by Räsänen and Ramstedt is not entirely clear phonetically. Cincius 1949: 163f. gives two examples of such a correspondence: Ma. *gabta-* 'shoot a bow' = Even, Evk., Nan., Sol., Ulč. *-rp-*, Mo. *-rv-* and Ma. *arfuku* 'мухогонка' = Even, Evk., Ulč. *-rp-*, both qoted by Benzing 1955: 48; but the derivation, and additionally the word *gabta-* are marked with a question mark (although the entire expression is unclear).

3   It seems to us that this proposition is relatively improbable. The word is not found beyond eastern Ir. languages, has no etymology there, and apparently no cognates, either. See below.

To our knowledge, the only exception here has been made by Tatarincev 2000– who submitted his own – and more importantly a very probable – proposition: **ar-* 'multiply oneself, be numerous' + *-p* intensification + *-a*, cf. OTkc. *arka* 'multitude; collection; crowd; group', Mo. *arbin* 'plentiful' et al.

Possibly, an interesting addition to this hypotheses might be made of OJap. **apa* 'millet' (Martin 1987: 388, Omodaka 2000)[4] which, it seems, may be genetically related to the Tkc. form – and then to the Mo. and Ma. ones, too. If this was indeed true, it would give added weight to Tatarincev's proposition.

It remains to be determined whether Pashto *orbəša* &c. are borrowings from Tkc. (not very plausible for cultural-historical reasons but definitely not impossible[5]), another realization of a much older cultural wanderwort of unknown origin (which seems to be quite probable but is absolutely impossible to determine, at least for now)[6], or whether the similarity of these words is a pure coincidence. The current state of art does not allow for a final answer.

ARPAGAN

FORMS:

arpagan OTkc.: Dmitrieva 1972 'wild barley' || Tat.: ÈSTJa 'wild barley; a plant similar to barley', Dmitrieva 1972 || Trkm.: Dmitrieva 1972 'agropyron'
arpagān MTkc.MK: Dankoff/Kelly 1982–85 'a plant similar to barley'
arpakan Kirg.: ÈSTJa 'wild barley; common wild oat (Avena fatua)'

LANGUAGES:

Kirg.: *arpakan* || MTkc.MK: *arpagān* || OTkc.: *arpagan* || Tat.: *arpagan* || Trkm.: *arpagan*

ETYMOLOGY:

1974: ÈSTJa: < *arpa* 'barley' + *-gan*

COMMENTARY:

This form has a very clear structure. *-gan* is quite a popular suffix for plant names, here with a distinct meaning of 'similar to, such as'. Cf. *arpakan* 'oats'.

The MTkc.MK long *-ā* in the suffix is supposedly a transcription of alef, and not an actual length of the vowel, otherwise completely incomprehensible.

---

4   This word is attested as early as the oldest Jap. monument, Man'yōshū (8th c.). Interestingly enough, it is written with the 粟 sign, nowadays used for Mand. *sù* < MChin. *sjowk* > OTkc. and others *sök* 'millet' (cf.).

5   If so, then probably from a Px3Sg form (in a compound?).

6   Such a solution should also be considered for Hung. *árpa*, whose origin from Čuv. is not likely for phonetic reasons (Čuv. *o/u-* vs Hung. *á-*). From among the possible sources quoted in EWU, Com. *arpa* seems to be most probable phonetically and cultural-historically but perhaps other sources with non-Čuv. sounding can not be entirely excluded, too.

AS

FORMS:
as **Khak.**: Dmitrieva 1972
aš **Brb.**: R I 585b || Šr. R I 585b
LANGUAGES:
Brb.: *aš* || **Khak.**: *as* || **Šr.**: *aš*
ETYMOLOGY:
   1974: ÈSTJA: < Ir. *āš* 'soup'
COMMENTARY:
   Corresponds with Tkc. *aš* 'food' et al., including Khak., Kmk. 'cereal'; Oyr., Tat.dial. 'cereal in ears and the like'; Khak., Oyr. 'grain', presumably < Ir. (ÈSTJa). The word appears in many Tkc. languages in different meanings (ÈSTJa) which can be reduced to three groups: 1. 'soup', 'pilaff'; 2. 'food, nourishment', and 3. 'cereal', 'grain'. ÈSTJa believes the first group to be a Čag. innovation (even though such a meaning is attested in MIr. where the word originates from), the second group represents the original meaning (this is the only meaning attested in older Tkc. monuments), and the third one to be a later concretization of meaning 2. (it only appears in Brb., Khak., Kmk., Oyr., Tat.dial. and Šr.).

   In the oldest monuments, the word is only attested in the meaning of 'food, nourishment' (ÈSTJa). However, it does not seem to be very probable that such a meaning would evolve into 'cereal', 'grain' and so on in Khak., Kmk., Oyr., Tat.dial. &c. We would rather believe that it is these languages that preserved the original meaning from before the OTkc. period. This hint, together with the commonness of the word in Tkc. could suggest that its relationship to Ir. *aš* 'kind of soup' has just the opposite direction than the one suggested by ÈSTJa. However, the Ir. word has an established etymology: Pers. *āš* < Skr. *āśa* 'food, nourishment' (Turner 1966–69: 66), Skr. *aca-* in *prataraca-* 'breakfast', Av. *kahrkasa-* 'Hühnerfresser' (Horn 1893: 29). Thus, we should probably accept the slightly strange evolution from 'food' to 1. 'soup', 2. 'cereal', where 1. must have come into existence still in the OTkc. period.

   Whether Khak. has evolved the meaning of 'barley' from 'cereal; grain', or independently (i.e. from the original 'food, nourishment'), cannot be determined with certainty. The latter seems, however, to be more plausible because: 1. it has almost always been wheat and not barley, that was the most important cereal for the Tkc. peoples, and so we would rather expect 'cereal; grain' to evolve into 'wheat', rather than 'barley'; 2. barley was an important part of nourishment in the form of a gruel or a pulp; also, beer was made from it (Tryjarski 1993: 54, 123) which seems to point to the evolution from the meaning of 'soup' rather than 'cereal; grain'.

   Cf. *aš(lyk)* 'wheat'.

JAČMEŃ

FORMS: *jačmeń* **Tof.**: RTofS
ETYMOLOGY: as yet not discussed
COMMENTARY: < Russ. *jačmenь* id.

KÖČE

FORMS:

köče **Khak.**: RChakS, ÈSTJa, Tatarincev 2000
köže **Tuv.**: RTuwS, Tatarincev 2000

LANGUAGES:

Khak.: *köče* ‖ **Tuv.**: *köže*

ETYMOLOGY:

1974: ÈSTJa s.v. *köže*: < Pers. كوژه *gouže* 'Prunus divaricata Ledeb. [species of plum]'
2000: Tatarincev: < *köč- 'to reduce (oneself)'

COMMENTARY:

This word is quite common in the Tkc. languages in different meanings. Almost all of them are names of various dishes or their components (most often, flour) made of cereals (barley, corn, millet and wheat, very occasionally rice and sorghum as well), and only in a few cases of cereals or grains. In dialects other meanings sporadically appear, too (see below). A comprehensive list can be found in ÈSTJa.

The geographical distribution of the meanings does not seem to contribute much to our understanding. Only Tksh. dialects have all four meanings of the most important cereals at once, and only in eastern Siberia is there no other meaning present but 'barley'. Apart from Tksh. dialects, 'barley' appears in the North and East, 'corn' in the South, and 'millet' and 'wheat' in the centre, which corresponds quite precisely to the ranges of cultivation of these cereals. When taking all of this into account, one could try to suppose that all these meanings are relatively young, but it must not be forgotten that the word is attested in the Tkc. languages from the 14th c., and the choice of cereals for cultivation is mainly influenced by climate, which has not changed significantly in the last few centuries.

The etymology proposed by ÈSTJa does not seem to be grounded very well from the semantic point of view, as it assumes the following evolution: Pers. 'species of plum' [> **(a)** Tkc. 'mulberry fruits flour' > **(b)** 'flour made of roasted barley or wheat'] > **(c)** 'flour of various cereals' > **(d)** 'various dishes of cereals' &c., which is only supported by the following facts: 1. [in the Pamir. languages] 'mulberry fruits flour' and 'flour made of roasted barley or wheat' was designated by one word; 2. Uzb.dial., Tksh.dial. *gōža, köžötüt* 'species of mulberry'; 3. Uzb.dial. *gōža* 'species of plum'. While (c) > (d) is trivial, (a) is not very likely, and it must be remembered that (b) refers to the Pamir. languages, not Tkc. Whether the information that mulberry fruits flour became so popular in Pamir that it ousted flour made of cereals, also refers to Tkc. is unclear (cf. Steblin-Kamenskij 1982: 87, quoted by ÈSTJa). We believe that these difficulties provide sufficient reason to discard the etymology. The still unclear forms 2. and 3. may be understood as a quite strange evolution, probably under Pers. influence, especially in the case of 3.

Tatarincev 2000 is against this etymology, too.

Tatarincev's proposition seems to be much more likely. He derives *köče* < *köč-, and supports this reconstruction with words like Tkc. *g/küčük* 'puppy; young of an animal', also 'bud', *köš/ček* 'young of a camel', also 'young of an animal', and Tksh. *güžük* 'short; without tail', *göč(k)en* '(one year old) hare' and so on.

As to the derivation, it might be regarded as being problematic, that the word has a long vowel in Trkm. (*kȫže*). But a secondary evolution in Trkm. is possible, too – under the influence of Pers. *gou̯že*?

The reconstruction of **köč-* is very interesting but it seems to us that the examples listed by Tatarincev point quite clearly to the original meaning of 'to be small' rather than 'to reduce (oneself)'. Actually, this seems to fit *kȫže* even better (barley grains are quite small).

SULA

FORMS: *sula* **Tel.**: Ryumina-Sırkaşeva/Kuçigaşeva 1995
ETYMOLOGY: see *süle* 'oats'
COMMENTARY:
This word is one of the examples of the quite common identifying/confusing of 'barley' and 'oats': cf. commentary on *julaf* (point 2) and *arpakan*, *harva* and *tay arpasy* 'oats'. Only the direction is unclear here: this is the only word where 'barley' < 'oats'.

ŠAʿĪR

FORMS: *šaʿīr* **Ott.**: (شعير) Wiesentahl 1895, *šaʿīr* Redhouse 1921
ETYMOLOGY: as yet not discussed
COMMENTARY: < Arab. شَعِير *šaʿīr* 'barley'.

TAK-TAK

FORMS: *tak-tak* **Kzk.**: 'wild barley' DFKzk
ETYMOLOGY: as yet not discussed
COMMENTARY:
This name is completely obscure. Presumably, Kzk. *tak* '1. throne; 2. odd number' corresponds to Uyg. *tay* '1. mountain; 2. odd number', but the semantic relationship is utterly unclear. Also, the word has a strange structure which we cannot explain.
Cf. *tay-arpasy* 'oats'.

ŽEH

FORMS: *žeh* **Tksh.dial.**: Pisowicz 2000: 239
ETYMOLOGY: 2000: Pisowicz: 239: < Kurd. *žeh* 'barley'
COMMENTARY: We can see no flaw in the etymology presented by Pisowicz 2000: 239.

ŽEHIMIEN

FORMS:

nečimien **Yak.:** Pekarskij 1917–30, Anikin 2003

nehimien **Yak.:** Anikin 2003

ńečimien **Yak.:** Pekarskij 1917–30, Slepcov 1964: 37, 109, Anikin 2003

ńesemen [ɔ: -h-] **Yak.:** Pekarskij 1917–30, Anikin 2003

žesemen [ɔ: *žehemen*] **Yak.:** (жэсэмэн [ɔ: *ðь*-]) Dmitrieva 1972

žehimien **Yak.:** RJakS, Anikin 2003

žesemen [ɔ: -h-] **Yak.:** Pekarskij 1917–30, Anikin 2003

ETYMOLOGY:

1964: Slepcov: < Russ. *jačmeń* 'barley'

1972: Dmitrieva: < Russ. *jačmeń* 'barley'

2003: Anikin: Russ. *jačméń* (alternately. Sib. **jašméń*) > Yak. *žesemen* > other forms, cf. Ubrjatova 1960: 23 for *ž-* ~ *n-* / *ń-* , and indicates Russ. *člen* > Yak. *čilien*, *silien* for *-s-* ~ *-č-* and refers to Slepcov 1964: 109

COMMENTARY:

The etymology presented by Slepcov 1964 and more comprehensively by Anikin 2003 is undoubtedly true in general. However, it is unclear to us why Anikin 2003 believes that *žesemen* is the oldest form, from which *ńesemen* and *ńečimien* evolved by means of assimilation.

It seems that his reasoning is based solely on the sounding of these forms, but it is impossible to unambiguously settle the chronology of their borrowing, as assimilation depends not so much on the time of borrowing, as on how well the borrower knew Russian, and therefore it can only help to establish a chronology expressed in generations, not in absolute years; cf. Stachowski, M. 1999b: 23. The differences between the forms are: 1. anlaut (*ž-*, *n-*, *ń-*), 2. adaptation of Russ. *-s-* (*-h-*, *-č-*), 3. epentetic vowel (*-e-*, *-i-*) and 4. yielding or not of the Russ. accent (*-ie-*, *-e-*). From among these features only 3. lets us draw some conclusions regarding chronology: in the Tkc. languages epentetic vowels are high[7], and so *-e-* should be understood as a result of assimilation. We believe therefore that *jačmeń* > Yak. **Jačimien* > *Ječimien* > *Ječemen*. Regarding phonetics, cf. *ebies* 'oats'.

---

7   This is a constant feature of the Tkc. languages; cf. e.g. the necessity of Tkc. mediation in Hung. *király* 'king' << Southern Slav.dial. **kraľъ* or similar (Helimskij 2000: 434). Cf. also *aryš* 'rye'.

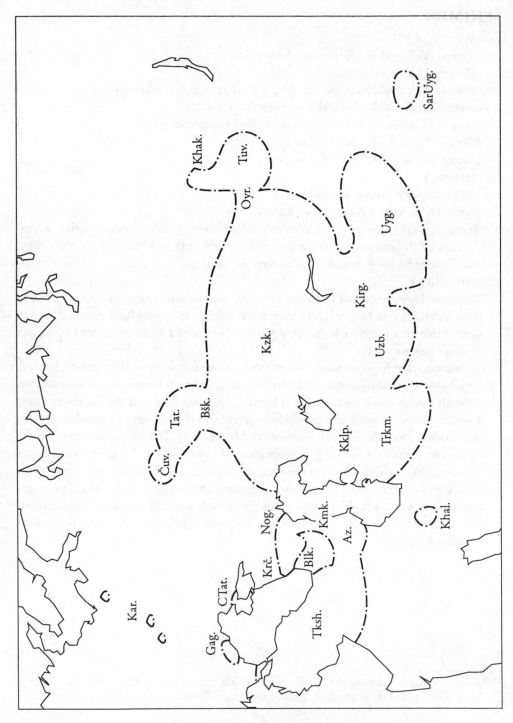

arpa 'barley'

CORN

ZEA MAYS L.

Corn originates from the Mesoamerican centre. The first traces of cultivation of corn were found in the Tehuacán valley, Mexico. They are dated around 5th millennium BC, while the domestication probably happened between 10th and 5th millennium BC. The oldest remains of cobs of a cultivated form are dated 3000–3500 years BC and were found in the fifties in Bat Cave, Mexico (cobs from these period are just 25 mm long). The oldest pollen of a wild form was discovered in the city of Mexico and is about 80 thousand years old. All presently known forms of corn are domesticated; wild forms have not survived at all.

Corn was extremely important for all the cultures of Central and South America, and was also known in North America. It appeared very often, and it still does, as a motif in art, and it played a role in mythology and religious rituals. Columbus mentioned it as early as 5 November 1492, and brought it to Europe a year later when he came back from his first voyage. From Spain (cultivations in Andalusia since 1525), it spread to Southern and Central Europe (Fr. *blé d'Espagne*, G. *Welschkorn*), and to Middle East and Anatolia from where it diffused further. Eastern and Central Europe (for the second time) learned about it later, from the Turks (cf. e.g. Slvn. *turščica*; Cz. *turkyně*; Pol. *pszenica turecka* and Fr. *blé de Turquie*, G. *türkischer Weizen* and *türkisch Korn*, It. *granturco* et al.). The Portuguese played a great role in its circulation by delivering it to Java as early as 1496, to Angola about 1500, to China in 1516 and to the Philippines in 1520 (Nowiński 1970: 193–202.)

The Latin name is a compound of Lat. *zēa* 'type of grain' + *mays* < Sp. *maís*, *máis* < *mahíz* < Taino *maisí*, *majisí* 'corn'. Fr. *maïs* and Eng. *maize* are borrowings from Spanish (Lokotsch 1926).

In the Tkc. languages there are altogether 16 different names for 'corn'. Nine of them are compounds built of an attribute + name of another plant, or are an abbreviation of this model. In three (four?) of them the attribute is a place name, always referring to an Arabic country (*Mäkke*, *Mısır*, *Şam*, ? *käbä bödoj*).

FORMS:

aži bijdaj	*kargi-dali* → *gargydaly*	*konag* → (*kömme*) *qonaq*
ažy bijdaj → *aži bijdaj*	*kokoroz*	*kukkurus* → *kokoroz*
basadohan	*köma qonaq* → (*kömme*) *qonaq*	*kukurus* → *kokoroz*
bordoq	*kömbö konok* → (*kömme*)	*kukurūsa* → *kokoroz*
čüžgün qonaq	*qonaq*	*kukurusь* → *kokoroz*
dary	*kömek* → (*kömme*) *qonaq*	*kukuruz* → *kokoroz*
gargydaly	*köme qonaq* → (*kömme*) *qonaq*	*kukuruza* → *kokoroz*
habiž(d)aj	*kömme qonaq*	*makkažavari* → *meke žügörü*
käbä bodaj → *käbä bödoj*	*kömür qonaq* → (*kömme*)	*makkažŭxori* → *meke žügörü*
käbä bödoj	*qonaq*	*makka(-)žuari* → *meke žügörü*

mäkke
mäkke žueri → meke žügörü
meke žügörü
mekgežöven
mekke ževen → mekgežöven
mokka-ʒavari → meke
   žügörü
mysir bogdaj → mysyr
   (bugdajy)

mysyr bogdaj → mysyr (bugdajy)
mysyr-bogdaj → mysyr
   (bugdajy)
mysyr bugdaj → mysyr
   (bugdajy)
mysyr (bugdajy)
nartük
nartux → nartük
nartüx → nartük

qonaq → (kömme) qonaq
sary
šam darysy
žasymyk
žügeri → žügörü
žügöri → žügörü
žügörü → žügörü
žŭxori → žügörü
žügeri → žügörü

LANGUAGES:

Az.: *gargydaly*
Bosn.Tksh.: *kukuruz*
Bšk.: *kukuruz* || *kukuruza*
CTat.: *mysir bogdaj*
Čuv.: *kukkurus* || *kukurusь*
   || *kukuruza*
KarC: *kokoroz* ||
   mysyr-bogdaj
KarH: *basadohan* || *sary*
Khak.: *kukuruza*
Kirg.: *meke žügörü* || *žügöri*
   || *žügörü* || *žügeri*
Kirg.dial.: *kömbö konok*
Kklp.: *mäkke* || *mäkke žueri*
Kmk.: *habiž(d)aj*

Krč.Blk.: *nartux* || *nartüx* ||
   žügeri
Kzk.: *žügeri*
Kzk.dial.: *žasymyk*
Nog.: *aži bijdaj* || *ažy bijdaj*
   || *nartük*
Ott.: *kokoroz* || *? mysyr bogdaj*
   || *? mysyr bugdaj* || *šam*
   darysy
Oyr.: *kukuruza*
Sal.: *konag*
Tat.: *käbä bodaj* || *käbä bödoj*
   || *kargi-dali* || *kukurus* ||
   kukuruz || *kukuruza*
Tksh.: *mysyr (bugdajy)*

Tksh.dial.: *dary* || *kokoroz* ||
   kukuruz
Trkm.: *mekgežöven* || *mekke*
   ževen
Tuv.: *kukuruza*
Uyg.: *bordoq* || *čüžgün qonaq*
   || *köma qonaq* || *kömek*
   || *köme qonaq* || *kömme*
   qonaq || *kömür qonaq* ||
   qonaq
Uzb.: *makkažavari* ||
   makkažŭhori || *makka(-)*
   žuari || *mokka-ʒavari* ||
   žŭxori
Yak.: *kukurūsa* || *kukuruza*

AŽI BIJDAJ

FORMS: *aži bijdaj* **Nog.:** RNogS || *ažy bijdaj* Dmitrieva 1972: 213
ETYMOLOGY: 1972: Dmitrieva: < *ažy* 'bitter' + *bijdaj* 'wheat'
COMMENTARY:

While it is not easy to present a convincing counterargument for the etymology proposed in Dmitrieva 1972, neither can one accept it without reservations. Semantics is definitely its weak point. Grains of wheat might indeed have a sweetish taste when compared to other cereals, but they certainly can not be regarded as sweeter than corn, which has a very distinct sweet flavour. Certainly it is not sweet enough to make it a distinctive feature.

Though we are not able to present a counterproposition, we do not want to accept Dmitrieva's solution, either. Not at least, in so brief a form. Perhaps she knows of more ethnographic data which could provide a more convincing argument in favour of her proposition.

BASADOHAN

FORMS: *basadohan* **KarH**: KRPS 105, Mardkowicz 1935 '1. corn; 2. corn gruel, polenta'
ETYMOLOGY: as yet not discussed
COMMENTARY:

We believe that this word is a compound of *basa* 'pasha' + *dohan* < Hebr. דוחן *dochan* 'millet'[8]. Millet is quite often unified or confused with corn (cf. *žasymyk*). Such a compound has a nice semantic parallel in Bulg. *carevica* 'corn'.

Cf. *cebedogon* 'millet'.

BORDOQ

FORMS: *bordoq* **Uyg.**: 'roasted corn'
ETYMOLOGY:

1974: ÈSTJa: Tkc. *bürtük* ~ *bürčük* '1. grain; 2. bread; 3. little bite; 4. et al.' < PTkc. **bürt-* 'come off, fall off'. The Uyg. form is not quoted here; all quoted forms (except for Čuv.) have vowels *e*, *i*, *ö* and *ü*

COMMENTARY:

Despite phonetic difficulties (front vs back vowels), we are convinced that this word belongs to the family of *bürtük*. A semantic shift from 'grain' to 'species of cereal' is absolutely natural; cf. e.g. Witczak 2003: 128–30. Cf. also Trkm. *bürdük* 'oats'.

ČÜŽGÜN QONAQ

FORMS: *čüžgün qonaq* جوزگون [sic] **Uyg.**: Jarring 1998: 15 'species of corn'
ETYMOLOGY: 1998: Jarring: 14: *ž* indicates a non-Tkc. origin; the word is enigmatic
COMMENTARY:

Jarring 1998: 15 only remarks that *ž* indicates a non-Tkc. origin, and that the word is enigmatic. He also mentions *čüžgün* 'green bristlegrass (*Setaria viridis*)' (after Schwarz 1992: 356) which is yet another example of calling 'corn' and 'millet' with one word (cf. *dary*, *mysyr bugdajy*, *žasmyk* and *žügörü*). It is not out of the question, that the word is etymologically identical with *čigin*, cf. *čüžgün* 'green bristlegrass (*Setaria viridis*)' in chapter Millet.

DARY

FORMS: *dary* **Tksh.dial.**: Tietze 2002–
ETYMOLOGY: see *dary* 'millet'
COMMENTARY: See *šam darysy* 'corn'.

---

8   Although it could alternately be Hebr. דגן *dagan* 'cereal'.

GARGYDALY

FORMS:

gargydaly **Az.**: RAzS, Dmitrieva 1972: 213

kargi-dali **Tat.**: قارقی دالی Tanievъ 1909

LANGUAGES:

Az.: *gargydaly* || **Tat.**: *kargi-dali*

ETYMOLOGY: 1972: Dmitrieva: < *gargy* 'reed' + *daly* 'its branch'

COMMENTARY:

The structure of this word is so clear, and the similarity of corn to reed so obvious that we can see no reason to question the etymology presented by Dmitrieva 1972.

HABIŽ(D)AJ

FORMS: *habiž(d)aj* **Kmk.**: Dmitrieva 1972: 213, RKmkS

ETYMOLOGY: as yet not discussed

COMMENTARY:

This word is unclear morphologically. It is possible that *-biž(d)aj* corresponds to Tkc. *bugdaj* 'wheat' (with a simplification of the consonant cluster). The *ha-* in anlaut remains however, utterly incomprehensible.

KÄBÄ BÖDOJ

FORMS: *käbä bödoj* **Tat.**: R IV 1714t || *käbä bodaj* Voskresenskij 1894

ETYMOLOGY: as yet not discussed

COMMENTARY:

This name is not entirely clear. Its second element, *bödoj* raises no doubts about its Tkc. origin (Tkc. *bugdaj* 'wheat'), even though its vocalism is not quite so comprehensible.

As to *käbä*, it seems most likely to us that it is in fact a place name, Kaaba. A very nice semantic parallel for such a naming is provided by Trkm. *mekgežöven* and similar names in Kirg., Kklp. and Uyg., Tksh. *mysyr bugdajy* and Ott. *šam darysy*. However, front vowels in this form remain a mystery to us.

Possibly, although this does not seem very likely, this word is identical with Tksh. *kaba* 'simple, coarse'?

Naming one species of cereal with the name of another one, and an attribute raises no doubts (corn was brought to the Tkc. peoples relatively late).

KOKOROZ

FORMS:

kokoroz **KarC**: 'roasted corn grains' Levi 1996 || **Ott.**: R II 509bقوقوروز, MiklTürkEl قوقورس,Redhouse 1921قوقوروس, قوقوروز, قوقوروز || **Tksh.**: Eren 1999

kukkurus **Čuv.**: RČuvS-A

kukurus **Tat.**: Dmitrieva 1972: 213

kukurūsa Yak.: Slepcov 1975 (from 1935)

kukurusъ Čuv.: Nikolъskij 1909

kukuruz **Bosn.Tksh.**: R II 897m || **Bšk.**: Dmitrieva 1972: 213 || **Tat.**: RTatS-D, RTatS-G || **Tksh.**: Eren 1999

kukuruza **Bšk.**: RBškS, Dmitrieva 1972 || **Čuv.**: Dmitrieva 1972: 213, RČuvS-A, RČuvS-D, RČuvS-E || **Khak.**: RChakS, Dmitrieva 1972: 213 || **Oyr.**: RAltS || **Tat.**: Dmitrieva 1972: 213 || **Tuv.**: Dmitrieva 1972: 213 || **Yak.**: RJakS, Dmitrieva 1972: 213, Slepcov 1975 (since 1935)

LANGUAGES:

Bosn.Tksh.: *kukuruz* || **Bšk.**: *kukuruz, kukuruza* || **Čuv.**: *kukkurus, kukurusъ, kukuruza* || **KarC.**: *kokoroz* || **Khak.**: *kukuruza* || **Ott.**: *kokoroz* || **Oyr.**: *kukuruza* || **Tat.**: *kukurus, kukuruz, kukuruza* || **Tksh.**: *kokoroz, kukuruz* || **Tuv.**: *kukuruza* || **Yak.**: *kukurūsa, kukuruza*

ETYMOLOGY:

1930: Nikolić[9]: Tkc. [? ɔ: Tksh.] *koku* (or *mum* for the form *mumuruz*) 'stink' + *uruz* 'rice' > 'rice of poor species'

This proposition is thoroughly false for the following reasons: 1. there is no such word in the Tkc. languages as *mum* 'stink'; 2. there is no such word in the Tkc. languages as *uruz* 'rice'; 3. a compound of two nouns in Nom. which would have this kind of a meaning is impossible in the Tkc. languages; 4. to the best of our knowledge, the Tkc. peoples never considered corn to be a worse kind of cereal (and neither did the Slavic peoples, cf. e.g. Bulg. *carevica* 'corn'), in fact, the exact opposite was true; 5. it is very hard to find a major similarity between corn and rice, and we know of no parallel for unifying these two meaning in the Tkc. languages.

1972: Dmitrieva: Tat. *kukurus*, Bšk. *kukuruz*; Bšk., Khak., Čuv., Yak., Oyr., Tat., Tuv. *kukuruza* < Russ.

1999: Eren: Tkc. *kokoroz* from the Balkan languages; cf. Bulg. *kukuruz*, Serb. *kukùruz*, Rom. *cucurúz*; ultimate source unclear

COMMENTARY:

We believe that this word was borrowed to the Tkc. languages from Slav., as Dmitrieva 1972 and Eren 1999 proposed it. In particular, the fact that the word has a very rich family in the Slav. languages and absolutely no relatives in the Tkc., speaks in favour of this proposition.

The sounding does not allow for a precise determination of the Slav. source. We can only make a guess based on historical and cultural-historical premises. In the case of Asian Tkc. languages it was most probably Russ.; in the case of Bosn.Tksh. we may suspect a borrowing from one of the Slav. languages of the Balkans or, less likely, from Tksh. (Ott.); and finally in the case of Tksh. (Ott.) – history seems to support the idea of a borrowing from the Balkans (as proposed by Eren 1999) rather than from Russ. (as Dmitrieva 1972 wants it).

All this might seem somewhat strange given the fact that Europe (except for Spain and Portugal[10]) has learned about corn from the Ottomans (see above). However, the

---

9 Nikolić, *Agronomski glasnik* 1930 and 1931; quoted after Skok 1971–74 s.v. *kukuruz*.

10 From Spain corn spread to France among other regions, and from there to Germany, but it only gained popularity later, probably under Turkish or Hungarian influence.

linguiśtic data does not allow for any other solution. Most probably, the whole thing might be explained by the following facts:

1. in Ott. (and later in Tksh.) the forms *kukuruz* ~ *kokoroz* are dialectal; corn was more popular among the Slavic people than it was among the Turks; in a limited area, a Slav. word could oust its Tkc. equivalent, and then find its way to the literary language
2. a) all the other Tkc. languages where this word is present, have been under a strong Russ. influence
   b) it is possible, that these Tkc. nations only learned about corn from Russians
The differences in auslaut among the Tkc. forms (-*uz* vs -*uza*) should probably be explained by variations in Russ. dialects (although Filin 1965– only attests *kukuróz*), or by a borrowing from Tksh. (Ott.) rather than from Russ.

The only thing that might still be regarded as being problematic is that our word has no established etymology in the Slav. languages. An overview of previous solutions (chronologically) and our proposition is presented below.

Blr.: *kukurúza* || **Bulg.**: *kukurùz* || **Cz.**: *kukuřice, kukuruc* (19th c.; Jungmann 1835–39[11]) || **Pol.**: *kukurydza* (20th c.), *kukurudza, kokoryca* (19th c.), *kukuryza, kukuruca, kukuryca, kukurudz* (18th c.) (SEJP) || **SC**: *kukùruz, kukùruza, kùkurica, kukuriza, kokuruz* (Skok 1971–74) || **Slvk.**: *kukurica, kukuruc* || **Slvn.**: *koruza* || **Ukr.**: *kukurúdza* || **USorb.**: *kukurica*

1. < Tkc. *kokoroz, kukuruz* 'corn'
   pro: Muchliński 1858[12]; MiklTEl, Karłowicz 1894–1905[13]; Lokotsch 1927; Weigand[14]; Holub/Lyer1967; Skok 1971–74; Witczak 2003: 124
   contra: MiklTElN; SEJP; Bańkowski 2000
   The word is incomprehensible on the Tkc. ground. Vast family in the Slav. languages. No related words in the Tkc. languages.
2. native word; cf. Slav.S. *kukurjav* '1. curly; 2. splayed out' (from 'hairs' protruding from corns)
   pro: Berneker 1908–13[15], Brückner 1927; Holub/Kopečný 1952; SEJP; Machek 1968; Zaimov 1957[16]; Schuster-Šewc 1978–89; ESUM; Černych 1993
   contra: Vasmer 1986–87
   See below.
3. < Rom. *cucuruz* '1. cone; 2. corn'
   pro: ? MiklFremdSlav, BER; Marynaŭ 1978–; ? Bańkowski 2000
   See below.
4. < *kukuru* used when luring birds with corn grains
   pro: Vasmer 1986–87

---

11   Jungmann 1835–39; quoted after Machek 1968.
12   Muchliński 1958: 71; quoted after SEJP s.v. *kukurydza*.
13   Karłowicz 1894–1905: 323; quoted after SEJP. s.v. *kukurydza*.
14   Weigand, G.: *Jahresbericht des Instituts für rumänische Sprache* XVII-XVIII: 363f.; quoted after SEJP.
15   Berneker 1908–13: 640–41; quoted after SEJP s.v. *kukurydza*.
16   Zaimov 1957: 113–26: 117–19; quoted after SEJP s.v. *kukurydza*.

contra: SEJP

Very unlikely. Would require an assumption that the name for 'corn' only came into existence after its grain had been acquired in some way, and used to lure birds while shouting (why?) *kukuru*. Apart from the above, it is not known which language the proposition refers to.

5. = ? Alb. *kúqur* 'baked; roasted' or = ? Alb. *kókërr* '1. grain of pea; 2. berry'

pro: Bańkowski 2000

Kókërr (< *kokë* 'head; bulb; berry; grain'; Orel 1998) seems to be more probable, but as a source of borrowing, rather than an equivalent. It also has, however, a very likely Slav. proposition (see below), this coincidence should probably be regarded as accidental. What is important, though, is the idea proposed by Bańkowski 2000 that the word might have been borrowed via two routes (see below).

SEJP suggests that the word should be derived from PSlav. **kokor-*, a reduplicated form of **kor-* (> **korenь*), such as *bóbr*, *gogołka* or *popiół*; cf. also *kąkol* 'corncockle (*Agrostemma githago*)[17]' and *kuklik* '*Geum urbanum* L.'[18]. In the Slav. languages there are very many names of plants with a very similar sounding, cf. e.g. Bulg. *kukurják* || Cz. *kokořík* || LSorb. *kokrik* || Pol. *kokornak, kokorycz* || Slvk. *kokorík, kukurík* || Ukr. *kokorička* || USorb. *kokorac* (more examples e.g. in SEJP s.v. *kokornak*). The semantic basis were most probably curly (crooked?) leaves or tendrils, or some kind of curls or 'locks' characteristic of the given plant (cf. Machek 1968; SEJP). Cf. Slav.S. *kukurjav* 'curly(-headed)'[19].

We believe that PSlav. **kor-* 'bent' can with quite a high degree of probability be accepted as the root of our word: cf. also Russ.dial. *kokóra* 'trunk [...] together with a crooked root [...]', Hung.dial. *kukora* 'crooked; bent; [...]'[20], and Pol. and others *krzywy* 'crooked', maybe also Lat. *curvus*.

Many Slavists point out phonetical difficulties. Two routes of borrowing, proposed by Bańkowski 2000, seem to offer the best explanation. Only instead of the Alb. etymons, we would rather assume native Slav. names either shifted from another similar plant, or neologisms created in the same way as the already existing names. Presumably, some of the forms may be explained by a contamination of two (or more?) forms (for Pol., cf. Bańkowski 2000).

---

17 NB: Probably also Hung. *kankalék* 'primrose' (in the same way as *konkoly* 'corncockle') is a borrowing from the Slav. languages – against EWU, where it is regarded as an 'Abl[eitung] aus einem fiktiven Stamm, Entstehungsweise aber unbest[immt]'. Cf. also Lith. *kānkalas* '(little) bell, something clanging' (Spólnik 1990: 64).

18 From Cz., where it meant among others 'monk's hood'; cf. Spólnik 1990: 84, though an unclear expression.

19 Also Hung. *kökürü* 'curly(-headed)', which probably from the Slav. languages, too – against EWU, where it is derived from *kukora* 'crooked, bent, [...]', which is an 'Abl[eitung] aus einem relativen fiktiven Stamm'.

20 See footnotes 17–19. Cf. Pol. *kąkol* 'corncockle (*Agrostemma githago*)' of a very similar structure.

Finally, we should also consider whether it would be desirable to assume a Paleo-Europ. source, which could be connected with OBask. and Pre-Romance **kuk(k)ur-* 'Kamm; Spitze' (more: Hubschmid 1965: 39), and the Rom. form (originally 'cone'), instead of deriving it directly from Bulg. (cf. Cihac 1879: II 86 vs. Cioranescu 1966). An Ott. meaning attested by Redhouse 1921: 'any tall, ill-shaped thing', might also be used to support this idea. We suppose that Arm. *gogaṙ* and the like. 'hooks with two points used for hanging pots over a fire' (Bläsing 1992: 58) could also belong to the same family, such as finally. Tksh. *kokoreç* 'meat dish roasted on spit'.

(KÖMME) QONAQ

FORMS:

köma qonaq Uyg.: (Turfan) Jarring 1998: 14
kömbö konok Kirg.dial.: ÈSTJa 'corn'
kömek Uyg.: Jarring 1998: 14 'special species of corn'
köme qonaq Uyg.: Jarring 1998: 14 'special species of corn'
kömme qonaq Uyg.: كومه قوناق RUjgS, Jarring 1998: 14 'special species of corn'
kömür qonaq Uyg.: Jarring 1998: 14
konag Sal.: ÈSTJa
qonaq قوناق Uyg.: Raquette 1927, ÈSTJa

LANGUAGES:

Kirg.dial.: *kömbö konok* ‖ **Sal.:** *konag* ‖ **Uyg.:** *köma qonaq, kömek, köme qonaq, kömme qonaq, kömür qonaq, qonaq*

ETYMOLOGY:

1998: Jarring: 14: ? *kömme* < *köme* ~ *kömer* 'coal' (cf. *kömür qonaq*), or ? *kömme* < *kömek* '?'

COMMENTARY:

KÖMME:

Jarring's 1998: 14 proposition which is based on the form *kömür qonaq*, and derives *kömme* from *kömür* (~ Uyg. *köme(r)*) 'coal' is interesting but, semantically, rather enigmatic.

It seems more plausible to us that *kömme* is a deverbal noun from the verb *köm-* 'to bury, dig in the ground'. Such an attribute may result from the way corn is planted: rather than simply sowing seeds onto ploughed ground, its seeds are thrown into specially prepared pits, and then covered with soil. For semantics, cf. also the somewhat enigmatic in this regard, *sokpa*. Although this proposition does not explain forms with -*r* in auslaut, which still remain incomprehensible to us, it still, nonetheless, seems be more plausible.

It is probable that the same root that can be found in Tkc. *kömeč* '1. bread; 2. pie; dumpling'.

QONAQ: See *konak* 'millet'.

MÄKKE

FORMS: *mäkke* (plant and dish) **Kklp.:** RKklpS-B, RKklpS-BB, RKklpS-ST
ETYMOLOGY: see *meke žügörü* and *mekgežöven*

COMMENTARY:

Mäkke as a name for 'corn' is certainly an abbreviation of *mäkke žueri*, created by the same token as *mysyr buğdajy* > *mysyr* in Tksh. According to Dmitrieva's 1972 explanation, it means 'Mecca' – cf. Kirg. *meke* among others 'Mecca', and comes from Arab. *makka* مكة (quoted by Dmitrieva as *Meke* s.v. *meke žügörü*, and as *Mekke* s.v. *mekgeǯöven*).

Cf. *meke žügörü* and *mekgeǯöven*, and *mysyr buğdajy* and *šam darysy*.

MEKE ŽÜGÖRÜ

FORMS:

makkažavari **Uzb.:** مكه جوارى Nalivkinъ 1895
makkažŭxori **Uzb.:** RUzbS-A, RUzbS-Š
makka(-)ǯuari **Uzb.:** Lapin 1899, Smolenskij 1912
mäkke žueri **Kklp.:** RKklpS-BB
meke žügörü **Kirg.:** Dmitrieva 1972: 213, RKirgS-Ju44, RKirgS-Ju57
mokka-ǯavari **Uzb.:** Smolenskij 1912

LANGUAGES:

Kirg.: *meke žügörü* || **Kklp.:** *mäkke žueri* || **Uzb.:** *makkažavari, makkažŭhori, makka(-)ǯuari, mokka-ǯavari*

ETYMOLOGY: 1972: Dmitrieva: < Arab. *Meke* 'Mecca' + *žügörü* 'corn'

COMMENTARY:

MEKE: See *mäkke*.

ŽÜGÖRÜ: See *žügörü*.

Cf. *mäkke, mekgeǯöven*, and *mysyr buğdajy* and *šam darysy*.

MEKGEǮÖVEN

FORMS:

mekgeǯöven **Trkm.:** Dmitrieva 1972: 213, Nikitin/Kerbabaev 1962, RTrkmS
mekke ǯeven **Trkm.:** Alijiv/Böörijif 1929

ETYMOLOGY: 1972: Dmitrieva: < *mekge* < Arab. *Mekke* 'Mecca' + *ǯöven*

COMMENTARY:

MEKGE-: See *mäkke* and *mäkke žügörü*.

-ǮÖVEN:

This word is etymologically unclear. Though not listed among equivalents by Eren 1999, it is presumably the same word as Tksh.: *çöven* 'kökü ve dalları sabun gibi köpürten bir bitki' < *çöğen* Eren 1999, dial. *çoğan, çoğen, çovan, cöiven, çuvan* DS || Az. *çoğan* || OKipč. *çoğan* || Trkm. *çoğan (kökü)* 'çöven'.

We believe that it might be closely related to *čigin* 'millet', which unfortunately is unclear, too. We should not completely discount the notion that its ultimate source is Pers. *žoụ-* 'barley' (see *julaf* 'oats'), or alternately, that *čigin* < *čüžgün* – which would probably rule out such a connection.

Cf. *mäkke, mekgeǯöven*, and *mysyr buğdajy* and *šam darysy*.

MYSYR (BUGDAJY)

FORMS:

mysir bogdaj   CTat.: Zaatovъ 1906
mysyr bogdaj   ? Ott.: مصر بوغدای Wiesentahl 1895
mysyr-bogdaj   KarC: Levi 1996: 45
mysyr bugdaj   ? Ott.: مصر بوغدای Wiesentahl 1895
mysyr (bugdajy)   Tksh.: Dmitrieva 1972: 213

LANGUAGES:

CTat.: *mysir bogdaj* ‖ KarC.: *mysyr-bogdaj* ‖ Ott.: *? mysyr bogdaj, ? mysyr bugdaj* ‖ Tksh.: *mysyr (bugdajy)*

ETYMOLOGY:

1972:   Dmitrieva: < Arab. *Misr* 'Egypt'
1999:   Eren: does not explain the word – presumably, because he assumes it is obvious – that this name is a compound of a place name + a name of another plant (cereal), i.e. *mysyr bugdajy* liter. 'Egyptian wheat'
2000:   Bańkowski s.v. *kukurydza*: Tksh. *mysyr* < common Europ. *mais* (Sp. *maís*, Fr. *maïs* et al.)

COMMENTARY:

Bańkowski's 2000 proposition seems to be deeply problematic for serious phonetical and historical reasons. We think that a much better solution has been presented by Dmitrieva, and we believe, that also Eren implied that he had the same solution.

Currently, an abbreviation of *mysyr bugdajy* to *mysyr* caught on in Tksh., just as Kklp. *mäkke žueri* > *mäkke*. Cf. *šam darysy*, and *mäkke, meke žügörü* and *mekgežöven*.

An exact semantic parallel (a calque from Ott.?) is offered by Arm. *egipt-a-c'oren* 'corn', liter. 'Egyptian wheat'.

It remains somewhat enigmatic to us why this name has been formed with the help of a word for 'wheat' if in all the other compounds of this kind, a word for 'barley' has been used. Interestingly enough, in dialects *mysyr bugdajy* might actually mean 'barley', too: cf. *mysyr* 'barley' and *dary, jasymuk* and *jügür* id.

NARTÜK

FORMS:

nartük   Nog.: Dmitrieva 1972: 213, RNogS
nartux   Krč.Blk.: Dmitrieva 1972: 213
nartüx   Krč.Blk.: RKrčBlkS

LANGUAGES:

Krč.Blk.: *nartux, nartüx* ‖ Nog.: *nartük*

ETYMOLOGY: as yet not discussed

COMMENTARY:

This word is etymologically incomprehensible. We can see two ways of trying to explain it, but neither of them is anything more than a conjecture, and none of them is fully clear. However, the first seems to be more probable:

1. Osset. *nartxor* 'corn', liter. 'food of the Narts'[21]

   Semantically, such a connection raises no doubts. It is, however, quite inexplicable phonetically. One might believe that it is a Tkc. derivative from *nart 'Nart' with a meaning calqued from Osset. *nartxor*, but a non-harmonic vocalization undermines this solution.

2. common Europ. *nard*

   The word nard is present in many European languages (Lat. *nardus*, Eng., Fr., Pol., Russ. et al. *nard*) but to the best of our knowledge, it has no etymology. The plant originates from the region of India and Tibet, and has been known to Europeans since antiquity as a material for perfume production. It does not look similar to corn, but it should be remembered that 'corn' happens to be the same word for 'millet' (see *čüzgün qonaq, mysyr bugdajy, žasymyk* and *žügörü*), and that the popular terms for 'millet' might in fact mean various, not necessarily closely, related species (see commentary on 'millet'). A distant analogy is that *čikin* 'millet' may also mean 'French lavender'[22], and the word *nard* is not always entirely monosemantic as well, e.g. Gr. *νάρδος*, except for *Nardostachys Jatamansi* might in various compounds also mean 'Valeriana Celtica', 'Cymbopogon Iwaraneusa', or 'nard oil' (Lidell ⁹1968) and others.

SARY

FORMS: *sary* **KarH**: KRPS

ETYMOLOGY: as yet not discussed

COMMENTARY: From corn's extremely distinct colour.

ŠAM DARYSY

FORMS: *šam darysy* **Ott.**: Eren 1999 s.v. *mysyr*

ETYMOLOGY: as yet not discussed

COMMENTARY:

Cf. *mysyr buğdajy*, and *mäkke, meke žügörü* and *mekgežöven*.

For a comparison to millet, cf. *dary* and *mysyr bugdajy*, and *čüzgün qonaq, žasymyk* and *žügörü*.

---

21 The Narts were a race of giants described in the mythology of the peoples of Caucasus, including the Ossetians. According to the legends, a long time ago, out of pride they rose against God. God punished them by sending upon them a terrible famine. At night, they would shoot with their bows grains glittering in the sky and eat them but there were not enough, and eventually the entire race starved to death. After that, the grains fell to the ground and corn sprouted from them. (Dumézil 1930: 14)

Other languages of Caucasus might also be taken into consideration, see Dumézil 1930: 11: 'Peut-être qu'on songe que dans une bonne partie du Caucase du nord [...] le maïs, n'a d'autre nom que « l'aliment des Nartes »'.

22 The expression in Clauson 1972 is not entirely clear to us: 'ç̌iki:n [...] (3) the name of a plant called *usṭūxūdūs* 'French lavender' [...]; *çekin* same translation; [....]'.

ŽASYMYK

FORMS: *žasymyk* **Kzk.dial.**: ÈSTJa
ETYMOLOGY: see *jasymuk* 'millet'
COMMENTARY:

For naming 'corn' and 'millet' with one word, cf. *dary, šam darysy* and *žügörü*, and *čüžgün qonaq*.

ŽÜGÖRÜ

FORMS:

žügeri **Krč.Blk.**: Dmitrieva 1972: 213 || **Kzk.**: Dmitrieva 1972: 213, DFKzk, DKzkF, RKzkS-46, RKzkS-54

žügöri **Kirg.**: Mašanovъ 1899

žügörü **Kirg.**: Dmitrieva 1972: 213, RKirgS-Ju44, RKirgS-Ju57

žŭxori **Uzb.**: Dmitrieva 1972: 213

žügeri **Krč.Blk.**: RKrčBlkS

LANGUAGES:

Kirg.: *žügöri, žügörü, žügeri* || **Krč.Blk.**: *žügeri* || **Kzk.**: *žügeri* || **Uzb.**: *žŭxori*

ETYMOLOGY:

1972: Dmitrieva: only points to a connection with OTkc. *jügür, jür, ügür, üjür* and Čuv. *vir* 'millet', and with Oyr. *üre* 'кашица из толченой крупы', Tat. *öjrä, üre* 'кашица; крупяной суп', Mo. *ür* 'grain; seeds', OTkc. *jügürgün* 'plant similar to millet'

COMMENTARY:

Žügörü as a name for 'corn' is presumably an abbreviation of *meke žügörü* (cf. also *mekge-žöven*). Similarly *mäkke*.

However, the word is not entirely clear from the etymological point of view. The -*ü* in auslaut is probably a possessive suffix which originally created the so-called second izafet in compounds such as Kirg. *meke žügörü* – cf. Tksh.dial. *cögür* 'species of grass' DS, and Tksh. *mysyr bugdajy* 'corn' and Ott. *šam darysy* id. Eren 1999, Tksh.dial. *dary* TS. We believe that Dmitrieva's 1972 proposition to connect the word with OTkc. *ügür* &c. has much to commend it (see *ügür* 'millet').

Cf. *meke žügörü*.

kokoroz 'corn'

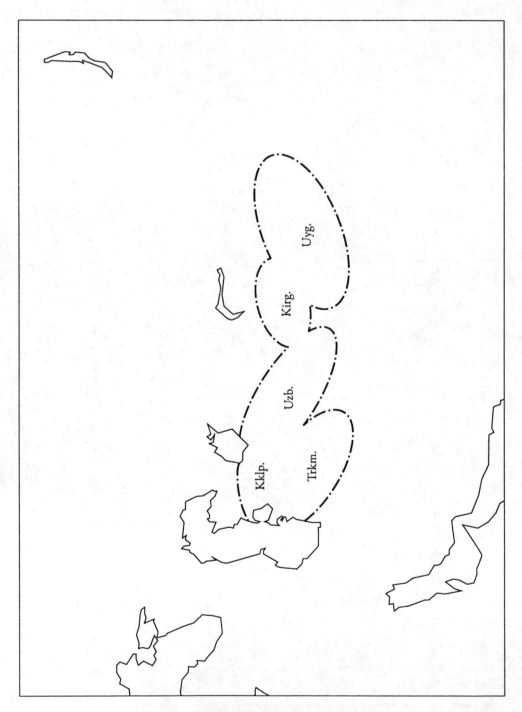

mäkke, meke žügörü and *mekgežöven* 'corn'

Millet is one of the first plants ever to be cultivated by mankind. It is understandable then, that the name for 'millet' encompasses in colloquial use many different, and not necessarily closely related species (see below). India, Central Asia, China and Africa's tropical savannahs are considered to be the homeland of millet. An exact dating of the beginnings of cultivation is very difficult, as distinguishing separate species in the archeological materials raises serious problems. In Europe, which is not the homeland of this cereal (or rather, cereals), it has been discovered in neolithic finds, and in China it had already been one of the five most important cereals sown by the emperor himself during the vernal equinox as early as in the 28th c. BC.[23] Proso millet has been traditionally cultivated in China, Central Asia, Turkestan and Transcaucasus.

The two most important species are colloquially both called millet: proso millet (*Panicum miliaceum* L.) and setarias, especially foxtail millet (*Setaria italica* P.B. = *Panicum italicum* L. and others). Also, some species of sorghum are sometimes called millet, too. Both the colloquial and even the botanical terminology is somewhat in confusion (see table in Nowiński 1970: 186), mainly because of numerous synonyms and polysemantic names. There is no reason to believe that the situation is any clearer in the Tkc. languages.[24] We believe that some of the names we list with the meaning of 'millet' refer in fact to some other species than proso millet, or that they refer to many species at once. Unfortunately, the lexical data we have had access to usually does not allow us to make these kinds of distinctions.

The lexical data itself does not let us determine whether it was millet or wheat that was the first cereal the Tkc. peoples became acquainted with. The fact that we know of no examples of a semantic shift 'millet' > 'wheat', and that we know of two examples in the opposite direction (unfortunately, both non-Tkc.: Nan. *būda* 'millet', Žu-čen *pùh-tuu-kai* 'millet' as opposed to Tkc. *bugdaj* 'wheat' (Joki 1952: 107)) might suggest that it was wheat that came first.

Interestingly, names for 'millet' are sometimes mixed or unified with names for 'corn' (cf. *čüž-gün, dary, jasymuk, jügür* and *mysyr*). Possibly, it results from the fact that the grains of these two cereals are similar to each other, both in shape and colour, though the grains of millet are smaller and flatter. It is also possible, perhaps even more probable, that this unification arose from the fact that corn had in many regions become the most important cereal, thus taking, at least to some extent, the place of millet.[25] One could suppose, for historical reasons, that the direction of the shift would always be 'millet' > 'corn' but this is not the case with *mysyr* (see below).

---

23 This refers to both the most important species: proso and foxtail millet (see below).

24 In fact, it is just the opposite: many of the names we list have a meaning such as 'a species of millet' or 'a plant similar to millet' &c.

25 Cf. also e.g. Pol. *burak* 'borago' > 'beetroot' resulting from beetroot's displacing borago and taking over its place (Boryś 2005).

FORMS:

cebedogon
čäkin → čigin
čigin
čigit → čigin
čikin → čigin
čingetarā → tarā
čüžgün
čygyt → čigin
darā → tarā
dari → dary
daru → dary
dary
indäü
itkonak → konak
jasymuk
jögür → ügür
josmik → jasymuk
jügür → ügür
jügürgün → ügür
jügürgǘn → ügür
jür → ügür
kojak → konak
konag → konak
konaɣ → konak
konak
konāk → konak
konakaj → konak
konok → konak

kunak → konak
mysyr
mysyr buğdajy → mysyr
mysyrda(ry) → mysyr
mysyrgan → mysyr
nardan
ögür → ügür
öjür → ügür
prosa
proso
qonaq → konak
qunoq → konak
sök
sokpa
sük → sök
tarā
taragan
taraɣ → dary
taran → taragan
tarān → taragan
tari → dary
tarī → dary
tarig → dary
tarik → dary
tariq → dary
taru → dary
tarū → dary
tary → dary

taryg → dary
taryɣ → dary
taryk → dary
teri → dary
teriɣ → dary
terik → dary
teriq → dary
tögi → tögü
tögü
töhö → tögü
tügä → tögü
tügi → tögü
tügü → tögü
tui → tögü
tüi → tögü
tüjtary
tyrǎ → dary
? tyryq → dary
ügür
ügürgǟn → ügür
üjür → ügür
*üör → ügür
ǖr → ügür
vir → ügür
xonak → konak
xōtarā → tarā
žavers

LANGUAGES:

Az.: dary
Blk.: tary
Brb.: taran
Bšk.: tary
Com.: tary [tari]
CTat.: dary
Čag.: čäkin || čigin || indäü
    || konag || konak || sök ||
    tarig || tarik || taryg || tügi
Čuv.: tyrǎ || vir
Fuyü: nardan
Gag.: dary

KarC: dary || tary
KarH: cebedogon
Khak.: prosa || taryg
Kirg.: konak || konok || tarū
    || tary
Kklp.: konak || tary
Kmk.: tari || tarī || tary
Kmnd.: taragan
Krč.: tary || tüi
Krč.Blk.: tary
Kzk.: itkonak || konak || sök
    || tary || tüjtary

MTkc.: čikin || jögür || jügür
    || kojak || konak || ögür
    || öjür || taryg || taryk ||
    tügi || ügür
MTkc.H: tary
MTkc.IM: taryg
MTkc.KD: taru || tügü
MTkc.MA.B: kojak ||
    konak || konāk
MTkc.MK: jügür || jügürgǘn
    || taryg || tögi || tügi || ügür
    || ügürgǟn || üjür

Nog.: *konakaj* || *tary*
OTkc.: *čigit* || *jasymuk* ||
    jügürgün || *jür* || *kojak* ||
    konak || *sök* || *tarik* || *taryg*
    || *tögü* || *töhö* || *tügä* || *üjür*
Ott.: *čigit* || *čygyt* || *daru* ||
    dary || *tary* || *žavers*
OUyg.: *qonaq* || *taraɣ* || *ūr*
Oyr.: *taragan* || *tarān*
SarUyg.: *sokpa* || *taryg*
Tat.: *dari* || *sük* || *tary*

Tat.Gr.: *tary*
Tel.: *taragan* || *tarān* || *taru*
    || *tarū* || *tary*
Tksh.: *dary*
Tksh.dial.: *mysyr* || *mysyr*
    bugdajy || *mysyrda(ry)* ||
    mysyrgan
Tob.: *tary*
Tof.: *darā*
Trkm.: *dary* || *konak* || *taryg*
    || *tui*

Tuv.: *čingetarā* || *tarā* ||
    xonak || *xōtarā*
Uyg.: *čüžgün* || *konaɣ* ||
    konak || *konok* || *qonaq* ||
    sök || *tariq* || *taryɣ* || *teri*
    || *teriɣ* || *terik* || *teriq* ||
    tügi || ? *tyryq* || *üjür*
Uzb.: *čigin* || *josmik* || *konak*
    || *kunak* || *qunoq* || *tarik*
    || *tariq* || *taryk*
Yak.: *proso* || *tarān* || **üör*

CEBEDOGON

FORMS: *cebedogon* **KarH:** KRPS

ETYMOLOGY: as yet not discussed

COMMENTARY:

This name is unclear. Most probably it is a compound of *cebe* + *dogon*, where *dogon* < Hebr. דגן *dagan* 'cereal' or alternately דוחן *dochan* 'millet; millet groats'; *cebe* is however, unclear. Cf. *basadohan* 'corn'.

ČIGIN

FORMS:

čäkin **Čag.:** چیکین 'species of millet'

čigin **Čag.:** R III 2110m چیغین 'very fine millet', 'cotton seeds', R III 2114b چیکین 'species of millet', VEWT 107 'very fine millet', 'cotton seeds' || **Uzb.:** چیغین 'very fine millet', 'cotton seeds' R III 2110m

čigit **OTkc.:** VEWT 107 || **Ott.:** VEWT 107

čikin **MTkc.:** VEWT 'ährenbildende Futterpflanze, die zwischen Weinstöcken angepflanzt wird'

čygyt **Ott.:** VEWT 107

LANGUAGES:

Čag.: *čäkin, čigin* || **MTkc.:** *čikin* || **OTkc.:** *čigit* || **Ott.:** *čigit, čygyt* || **Uzb.:** *čigin*

ETYMOLOGY: as yet not proposed

COMMENTARY:

This name is unclear, and to the best of our knowledge no etymology has been proposed for it as yet. It seems to us that it might be etymologically the same word as unfortunately the equally unclear *žöven* in *mekgežöven* 'corn'. This is entirely possible both phonetically and semantically (for naming 'millet' and 'corn' with one word cf. *čüžgün*, *dary*, *jasymuk*, *jügür* and *mysyr*). If it turned out, however, even though it is not very likely that *žöven* << Pers. *žou̯-* (cf. *julaf* 'oats'), than the possibility of connecting *čigin* with *cüžgün* and *žöven* should probably be excluded.

ČÜŽGÜN

FORMS: *čüžgün* **Uyg.**: Jarring 1998: 14 (after Schwarz 356) '*Setaria viridis*'
ETYMOLOGY: 1998: Jarring: 14: ž indicates a non-Tkc. origin; enigmatic word
COMMENTARY:

Cf. *čüžgün qonaq* 'corn'.

This word is unclear. One cannot help noticing the phonetic similarity to *čigin* 'millet' (cf.) which is unclear, too. If these two words were to be related, *čüžgün* is probably the older form.

DARY

FORMS:

dari **Tat.**: داری Tanievъ 1909
daru **Ott.**: ÈSTJa
dary **Az.**: RAzS, VEWT, Dmitrieva 1972, ÈSTJa, Eren 1999 || **CTat.**: ÈSTJa || **Gag.**: ÈSTJa || **KarC**: ÈSTJa, KRPS, Levi 1996 || **Ott.**: (داری) Wiesentahl 1895, طاری, داری, ununpp R III 1627m, VEWT || **Tksh.**: Dmitrieva 1972, ÈSTJa, Eren 1999, Tietze 2002– || **Trkm.**: Alijiv/Böörijif 1929, RTrkmS, Nikitin/Kerbabaev 1962, VEWT, Dmitrieva 1972, ÈSTJa, Eren 1999
taraγ **OUyg.**: ÈSTJa
tari **Kmk.**: Dmitrieva 1972
tarī **Kmk.**: ÈSTJa
tariγ **Čag.**: تاریغ R III 850m, VEWT
tarik **Čag.**: تاریـق 'Ackerfeld' R III 850m, ÈSTJa || **OTkc.**: تاریـق R III 850m || **Uzb.**: Eren 1999
tariq **Uyg.**: Brands 1973: 33 || **Uzb.**: RUzbS-A, Dmitrieva 1972, Brands 1973: 33, ÈSTJa
taru **MTkc.KD**: تاروا || **Tel.**: Ryumina-Sırkaşeva 1995
tarū **Kirg.**: RKirgS-Ju44, RKirgS-Ju57, Dmitrieva 1972, Brands 1973: 33, ÈSTJa, Eren 1999 || **Tel.**: R III 851m, Eren 1999
tary **Blk.**: VEWT, Eren 1999 || **Bšk.**: RBškS, Dmitrieva 1972, ÈSTJa, Eren 1999 || **Com.**: [tari] Grønbech 1942, ÈSTJa, KWb 380 || **KarC**: KRPS, ÈSTJa, Levi 1996 || **Kirg.**: Mašanovъ 1899, ÈSTJa || **Kklp.**: RKklpS-BB, RKklpS-ST, RKklpS-B, Dmitrieva 1972, ÈSTJa, Eren 1999 || **Kmk.**: RKmkS || **Krč.**: VEWT || **Krč.Blk.**: RKrčBlkS, Dmitrieva 1972 || **Kzk.**: RKzkS-46, RKzkS-54, Dmitrieva 1972, ÈSTJa, KWb 380, DFKzk, DKzkF, Eren 1999 || **MTkc.H**: (طاری) || **Nog.**: RNogS, Dmitrieva 1972, ÈSTJa, Eren 1999 || **Ott.**: R III 986b || **Tat.**: R III 846m, III 1047m, IV 1857b, Voskresenskij 1894, Imanaevъ 1901, RTatS-D, RTatS-G, Dmitrieva 1972, ÈSTJa, KWb 380, Eren 1999 || **Tat.Gr.**: Podolsky 1981 || **Tel.**: R III 851m || **Tob.**: ÈSTJa
taryg **Čag.**: ÈSTJa || **Khak.**: ÈSTJa || **MTkc.**: ÈSTJa, VEWT '1. grain; 2. millet', Eren 1999 'sowing; plant; barley; wheat; grain' || **MTkc.IM** || **MTkc.MK**: Dankoff/ Kelly 1982–85 || **OTkc.**: Dmitrieva 1972 'millet; grain; grass, Eren 1999 'sowing' || **SarUyg.**: '1. grain; 2. millet' VEWT || **Trkm.**: (تاریق) Nalivkinъ 1895
taryγ **Uyg.**: VEWT '1. grain; 2. millet'

taryk MTkc.KD: طارغ || Uzb.: Lapin 1899, ('крупное') Smolenskij 1912
teri Uyg.: '1. grain; 2. millet' VEWT
teriy Uyg.: ÈSTJa
terik Uyg.: R III 850m, VEWT
teriq Uyg.: Menges 1933, تيريق RUjgS, Dmitrieva 1972
tyrǎ Čuv.: VEWT 'grain; millet', Eren 1999 'cereal'
? tyryq Uyg.: تريق Raquette 1927

LANGUAGES:

Az.: *dary* || Blk.: *tary* || Bšk.: *tary* || Com.: *tary* [tari] || CTat.: *dary* || Čag.: *tarig, tarik, taryg* || Čuv.: *tyrǎ* || Gag.: *dary* || KarC.: *dary, tary* || Khak.: *taryg* || Kirg.: *tarū, tary* || Kklp.: *tary* || Kmk.: *tari, tarī, tary* || Krč.: *tary* || Krč.Blk.: *tary* || Kzk.: *tary* || MTkc.: *taryg, taryk* || MTkc.H: *tary* || MTkc.IM: *taryg* || MTkc.KD: *taru* || MTkc.MK: *taryg* || Nog.: *tary* || OTkc.: *tarik, taryg* || Ott.: *daru, dary, tary* || OUyg.: *taray* || SarUyg.: *taryg* || Tat.: *dari, tary* || Tat.Gr.: *tary* || Tel.: *taru, tarū, tary* || Tksh.: *dary* || Tob.: *tary* || Trkm.: *dary, taryg* || Uyg.: *tariq, taryγ, teri, teriy, terik, teriq, ? tyryq* || Uzb.: *tarik, tariq, taryk*

ETYMOLOGY:

1960: VGAS 62: OTkc. *taryg* 'Ernte, Getreide' = Mo. *tarijan* 'Feld, Saat', MMo. *tarijad* 'Saaten, Getreide', Xlx. *tariā* 'Saat'

1969: VEWT: ~ Mo. *tarijan* 'sowing; cereal; land, soil; grain'

1972: Clauson: < *tary* 'to cultivate land'; *d-* by contamination with Pers. *dārū* 'medicine, drug'

1972: Dmitrieva: OTkc. *taryg* 'millet; grain; grass' < *tary* 'to sow' + *-g*

1974: ÈSTJa: 1. Forms without *-g*: < *tar-* 'to cultivate land; to sow' + *-y*; 2. Forms with *-g*: < *tar-y-* 'to sow' or like 1.

1979: Dmitrieva: < *tary* 'to sow' + *-yg* 'result, outcome'
Tuv. *tarā*, Oyr. *tarān*, Tat., Brb. *taran* 'millet' < Mo. *tarijan* 'grain', where *-ān* < *-γan*

1999: Eren: < *tary* '(ekin) ekmek' + *-ǧ*

2002: Tietze: < OTkc. *taryg* (after Clauson 1972)

COMMENTARY:

This word has relatively uniform meanings in all the languages (after ÈSTJa):

1. The form without *-g* apart from 'millet' can mean: 'grain', 'cereal', 'groats' and the like, and other cereals. All these meanings are understandable given the etymology and, except for the last group, are of a very limited range (at most one of the following languages: Oyr., Tof., Tuv.).
    For Tksh.dial. meaning of 'corn', cf. *mysyr*, the commentary at the beginning of this chapter, and *čüžgün, jasymuk* and *jügür*.

2. The form with *-g* means also 'wheat', 'barley', 'grain', 'cereal', 'fodder', 'sowing', 'crops', 'harvest', 'cultivation', 'descendant' and the like. All these meanings are older and, except for the last possibility which is not fully clear, understandable in view of the etymology.

The morphological structure of this word and its deverbal origin are quite obvious. The problematic part is the final vowel of the verbal stem (see *tara* and *taragan*). It has been, however, solved by ÈSTJa in a very convincing way by interpreting *-y ~ -a* as a denominal suffix and deriving the verbal *tary- ~ tara-* from nominal **tar* 'sowing; harvest; field', which at the same time explains *dary* (< *tar-*), *taryg* (< *tar-(y-)*) and such forms as Sag. and others *tarlay* 'fodder', and OUyg. *taray* 'cereal' and the like (< *tar-a-*). Cf. *tarā*, *taragan*.

The contamination with Pers. *dārū* 'medicine, drug' assumed by Clauson 1979 to explain the voiced anlaut in Oghuz. is, as has been justly remarked by ÈSTJa, not very likely (although it seems to us that the semantic difficulty, not mentioned by ÈSTJa, migh be even more important than the fact that the Pers. *dārū* is unknown to SW Tkc. languages), and moreover, absolutely superfluous since the voicing of occlusives in anlaut is a regular change in the Oghuz. languages, and the *d-* forms in Kipč. (KarC. and Tat.) may be easily, and with a very high degree of plausibility, explained by an Oghuz. influence or borrowing.[26]

For further bibliography cf. first of all ÈSTJa and Eren 1999.

Dmitireva 1979: 163 has suggested that the fact that this name derives from the verb 'to sow' might be regarded as a testimony that millet was the first cereal cultivated by the Tkc. peoples. But, it might also not be true since, she continues, D. *tarwe* 'wheat'. AS *tare* 'tare, vetch' et al. < [sic] OInd. *dūrvā* 'millet' < PIE **der-* 'to rip off; to skin'. This seems to us to be quite poor reasoning. OInd. and the Grmc. languages are only very remotely related with one another, and the fact that what originally was one word now has different meanings is not actually very surprising. The Tkc. languages are related much more closely, and *dary* has a very uniform meaning (with a few exceptions, see above) of 'millet'; only in a few of the languages does it include 'grain', 'cereal' and the like. The situation is then, quite different. However, even in these, much more favourable conditions we do not believe – as Dmitrieva apparently does – that it is possible to establish which was the first cereal cultivated by the Tkc. peoples using only the etymology of one word. One could equally well suppose that the first cereal was named with a borrowing rather than a native word, and such a guess could not be proved any more.

Cf. also (-)*tarā* and *taragan*.

INDÄÜ

FORMS:
indäü Čag.: اينداو '[...] родъ проса, изъ котораго приготовляется масло [...]' R I 1449m
ETYMOLOGY: R I 1449m: < *indä+-ü*
COMMENTARY:

The etymology offered by Radloff is rather odd. *indä* appears in various languages, but with the meaning of 'to call, to summon'. Thus, the semantic connection – if it even exists – would require a comprehensive commentary, which Radloff fails to provide. Regrettably, we cannot offer a more convincing proposition, either.

---

26 They could also be understood as the result of an assimilation to the next consonant, i.e. *t-r* > *d-r*, which is however not very convincing since such a change is characteristic of Oghuz., not Kipč. languages.

JASYMUK

FORMS:

jasymuk OTkc.: '? millet' DTS, Dmitrieva 1972, ÈSTJa
josmik Uzb.: ['?'] VEWT

LANGUAGES:

OTkc.: *jasymuk* || Uzb.: *josmik*

ETYMOLOGY:

1969: VEWT: Čag. *jasmuk* 'lentil' < *jasy* 'wide'
1972: Clauson: *jasymuk*, ? *jasmuk* 'a flat (seed)' < *jas-*
1974: ÈSTJa: < *jas-* 'to flatten' or *jasy* 'flat'
1991: Erdal: 101: < *jasy* 'flat'

COMMENTARY:

This word is quite common in the Tkc. languages. It has many meanings, the most basic definitely being 'lentil', and not 'millet'.[27]

Etymologically, there can be no doubt that the word is a derivative from *jas-* 'to flatten' or *jasy* 'flat'; what does raise doubts though, is whether it is a deverbal or a denominal derivative; for bibliography cf. ÈSTJa. We believe that the former is much less likely due to the fact that -*muk* is in fact a denominal suffix (see Erdal 1991: 100). Two-syllable forms are surely the result of dropping the high vowel in the middle syllable, which is a completely natural phenomenon in the Tkc. languages.

The meaning of 'millet' most probably results from the fact that the grains of millet are quite flat. Their shape can actually be used as an auxiliary argument for the denominal origin of the word: the suffix -*myk* with the meaning of 'low intensity of the feature' fits the shape of millet grains better than any other would.

Cf. also *jasmyk* 'wheat' and *žasymyk* 'corn'.

KONAK

FORMS:

itkonak Kzk.: DFKzk
kojak MTkc.: 'mediocre species of millet' VEWT || MTkc.MK: DTS, ÈSTJa ||
    OTkc.: Dmitrieva 1972 ||
konag Čag.: قوناغ 'species of millet' R II 538m; VEWT, ÈSTJa
konaɣ Uyg.: ÈSTJa
konak Čag.: قوناق 'родъ крупнаго проса' R II 535b; 'mediocre species of millet'
    VEWT || Kirg.: Dmitrieva 1972 || Kklp.: ÈSTJa || Kzk.: 'родъ крупнаго проса'
    R II 535b || MTkc.: 'mediocre species of millet' VEWT || MTkc.MK: Dankoff/
    Kelly 1982–85 || OTkc.: R II 535b قوناق 'родъ крупнаго проса'; VEWT 'mediocre

---

27 A comprehensive list is available in ÈSTJa. However, it does not contain some interesting related forms in -*mak*, such as: Khak. *naspax*, Tuv. *čašpak* 'pearl millet mixed with boiled potatoes or fat', Tat.dial. *jasmak* 'lentil' < *jas-* 'to flatten' (here the descent from *jasy* must be excluded due to a clearly deverbal character of -*mak*) (Stachowski, M. 1995: 151f.).

species of millet', Dmitrieva 1972 ‖ **Trkm.**: ÈSTJa ‖ **Uyg.**: 'mediocre species of millet' VEWT ‖ **Uzb.**: ÈSTJa

konāk **MTkc.MA.B**: Borovkov 1971: 106

konakaj **Nog.**: ÈSTJa

konok **Kirg.**: ÈSTJa '*Setaria italica var. mogharium* Alef.', Steblin-Kamenskij 1982: 36 '*Setaria italica var. mogharium* Alef.; setaria (*Setaria* P.B.); foxtail millet (*Setaria italica* P.B.)' ‖ **Uyg.**: VEWT

kunak **Uzb.**: ('мелкое') Smolenskij 1912

qonaq **OUyg.**: DTS 'species of millet', Steblin-Kamenskij 1982: 36 ‖ **Uyg.**: Jarring 1964, Steblin-Kamenskij 1982: 36

qunoq **Uzb.**: Dmitrieva 1972, Steblin-Kamenskij 1982: 36

xonak **Tuv.**: ÈSTJa '*Setaria viridis* P.B.'

LANGUAGES:

Čag.: *konag, konak* ‖ **Kirg.**: *konak, konok* ‖ **Kklp.**: *konak* ‖ **Kzk.**: *itkonak, konak* ‖ **MTkc.**: *kojak, konak* ‖ **MTkc.MA.B**: *konāk* ‖ **MTkc.MK**: *kojak, konak* ‖ **Nog.**: *konakaj* ‖ **OTkc.**: *kojak, konak* ‖ **OUyg.**: *qonaq* ‖ **Trkm.**: *konak* ‖ **Tuv.**: *xonak* ‖ **Uyg.**: *konaɣ, konak, konok, qonaq* ‖ **Uzb.**: *konak, kunak, qunoq*

ETYMOLOGY:

1969: VEWT: ~ Mo. *qonaɣ, qonuɣ* 'millet'

1974: ÈSTJa: limits himself to quoting two previous comparisons with Mo. against Clauson 1972

1976: KWb 185: only points to the comparison with *qonaɣ, qonuɣ*

COMMENTARY:

This word is common in the Tkc. languages and has many meanings[28], 'millet' being the most common one.

Clauson's 1972 etymology is, as ÈSTJa has stated, very improbable for phonetic (*konak*, not *kōnak) and semantic (*kōn-* 'to sit', not 'to seat') reasons. Unfortunately, no other etymology has been proposed, and we are not able to provide one, either.

About borrowing this word to the Pamir. languages, see Steblin-Kamenskij 1982: 35f.

MYSYR

FORMS:

mysyr **Tksh.dial.**: DS

mysyr bugdajy **Tksh.dial.**: 'millet' Eren 1999

mysyrda(ry) **Tksh.dial.**: DS

mysyrgan **Tksh.dial.**: DS

ETYMOLOGY: as yet not discussed in the meaning of 'millet'

---

28 Most of them are related to cereals – as a general term, or as the name of some species. Apart from 'millet', they are: 'setarias' (Tuv.), 'corn', 'sorghum' (Kirg.) and others (ÈSTJa). See also (*kömme*) *konak* 'corn'.

COMMENTARY:

Usually *mysyr* means 'corn' in Tksh. Using one word to name these two cereals often happens (see *čüžgün, dary, jasymuk* and *jügür*) but the direction is always natural from the historical point of view, i.e. 'millet' > 'corn'. To assume that some of the Anatolian Turks learned about millet from Egypt would be totally unrealistic, given the history of the cultivation of millet. Probably, the only acceptable guess would be that corn displaced or at least surpassed millet in importance in some regions of Turkey (which is quite likely), and hence the secondary meaning (cf. footnote 32). To some extent, such a scenario is pointed to by Tksh.dial. *mysyrda(ry)* and *mysyrgan* with a clear suffix *-gan* which is used very often to form names of plants, usually with the meaning of 'similar to; -like' (cf. *arpakan* 'oats' and *arpagan* '(wild) barley'). *Mysyr* itself is probably an abbreviation of one of these forms, or simply a shift from *mysyr* 'corn'.

NARDAN

FORMS: *nardan* **Fuyü:** Zhen-hua 1987
ETYMOLOGY: as yet not discussed
COMMENTARY:

Probably from Pers. *nārdān* 'pomegranate seeds; (= *nārdānag*) dried seeds of wild pomegranate used as a spice' (Rubinčik 1970), though the semantic is not entirely clear. A devisable connection with *nartük* 'corn' should probably be ruled out despite of some remote associations.

PROSA

FORMS: *prosa* **Khak.:** RChakS, Dmitrieva 1972, Brands 1973
ETYMOLOGY:
   1972: Dmitrieva: < Russ. *proso* 'millet'
   1973: Brands: < Russ. *proso* 'millet'
COMMENTARY:

The final *-a* might be a result of two possible events: 1. a phonetical, not graphical borrowing; 2. borrowing of the Gen. form used as Part.[29] It seems impossible to determine, which is more likely. In reality, probably both these factors were present at the same time and separating them would be but an artificial operation, which would result in a more methodical description of the change mechanism.

---

29 Similarly to e.g. Yak. *pruoška, boruoska,* Šr. *prašqa* &c. 'snuff' << Pol. *proszka* (Helimskij 1990: 41, Anikin 2003) || Dolg. *häldäj* 'herring' < Russ. *selъdej* Gen.Pl. < *selъdь* 'herring' (Stachowski, M. 1999b) || Tuv. *köpäk* 'kopeck' < Russ. *kopeek* Gen.Pl. < *kopejka* 'kopeck' (Pomorska 1995: 99) &c. The phenomenon is absolutely understandable, given that borrowings are usually made during conversation when Nom. is normally used less frequently than oblique cases, cf. also Yak. *ostolobuoj* < Russ. *stolóvoj* Gen., Praep. or Dat.Sg. < *stolóvaja* 'canteen' || Tuv. *laptū* 'kind of baseball' < Russ. (*igratъ v*) *laptú* (Pomorska 1995: 102 and 100 respectively) and others.

PROSO

FORMS: *proso* Yak.: RJakS, Dmitrieva 1972
ETYMOLOGY: 1972: Dmitrieva: < Russ. *proso* 'millet'
COMMENTARY:

It is difficult to criticise the etymology proposed by Dmitrieva 1972. A complete lack of assimilation (cf. *ebies* 'oats') indicates that the borrowing was made only very recently, or alternately that the orthography does not in fact render the actual Yak. pronunciation.

SÖK

FORMS:

sök Čag.: SKE 240 TMEN, VEWT 'husked millet' || Kzk.: SKE 240, TMEN, VEWT 'husked millet', DFKzk, DKzkF || OTkc.: VEWT 'husked millet' || Uyg.: SKE 240

sük Tat.: 'millet pap' VEWT

LANGUAGES:

Čag.: *sök* || Kzk.: *sök* || OTkc.: *sök* || Tat.: *sük* || Uyg.: *sök*

ETYMOLOGY:

1935: KWb: 333: = Mo. *sög*, Klmk. *sög* 'chassed millet'
1949: SKE 240: < Chin.
1963: TMEN: ? Tkc. < Pers. *sōk* 'ear of corn, beard of corn'
1969: VEWT: < Chin., KorS (after: SKE 240) *sok*
        = Mo. *sög* 'millet; spelt'

COMMENTARY:

This word appears also in Kirg., Kzk., Trkm., Uyg. and Uzb. meaning 'spelt'. The origin proposed by SKE 240 seems very likely (see below).

TMEN, reasoning from the fact that the word is only attested as late as Čag., suggests the possibility of a borrowing from Pers. *sōk* 'ear of corn, beard of corn' which would directly, or via Tkc. dialects, originate from Chin. This proposition can not be completely discounted[30], even though its seems to complicate the route of borrowing beyond what is necessary. That a word was not attested earlier than Čag. does not mean it did not exist before.

As has been proposed by TMEN, the Chin. etymon SKE 240 most probably meant is 粟[31] sù 'foxtail millet (*Setaria italica* P.B.)'. We believe that its MChin. sounding, **sjowk* (Baxter: 129, oral information from Prof. A. Vovin [Honolulu]), **siok⁴* (Tōdō 2001) raises no doubts about the phonetics, and neither about the meaning.

---

30 The change of harmony from back to front could be explained by the palatal pronunciation of *-k* in Pers. The semantic change could be explainable as easily.

31 The same sign is used to write OJap. **apa* 'millet' (Martin 1987: 388, Omodaka 2000), cf. *arpa* 'barley'.

SOKPA

FORMS: *sokpa* **SarUyg.**: Teniševb 1976
ETYMOLOGY: as yet not discussed
COMMENTARY:

While morphologically this word is absolutely clear (*sok-* 'to stick, to poke' + *-ma*), its meaning is quite strange. The literal meaning of *'seedling' indicates 'rice' or 'corn' rather than 'millet'. One could try to look for a semantic parallel in *tögü*[32] but the meaning of **tög-* 'to beat, to hit' enables an evolution to basically any cereal, and makes it impossible to compare with *sok-*. Perhaps this is an example of unifying/mixing 'millet' with 'corn' (cf. (*kömme*) *konak*)?

TARĀ

FORMS:

čingetarā **Tuv.**: RTuwS, Dmitrieva 1972
darā **Tof.**: ÈSTJa
tarā **Tuv.**: R II 135b (in: kara ~ 'black millet'), Brands 1973: 33, ÈSTJa
xōtarā **Tuv.**: RTuwS

LANGUAGES:

Tof.: *darā* || **Tuv.**: *čingetarā*, *tarā*, *xōtarā*

ETYMOLOGY:

1972: Dmitrieva: < Tuv. *činge* 'thin' + *tarā* 'grain; cereal'
1973: Brands: 33: < Mo. *tarijan*, *tarān* 'harvest; cereal'
1979: Dmitrieva: Tuv. *tarā*, Oyr. *tarān*, Brb., Tat. *taran* 'millet' < Mo. *tarijan* 'grain', where *-ān* < *-γan*

COMMENTARY:

TARĀ

As opposed to *tara(ga)n*, this form has no *-n* in auslaut, and thus it can be hardly expected to contain a trace of *-gan*, as has been proposed by Dmitrieva 1979, or that it is borrowed from Mo., as Brands 1973: 33 has suggested (cf. *taragan*). What seems much more probable is that they are *-g* derivatives from *tar-a-*. For. *tar-a-* and the semantic of OUyg. forms cf. ÈSTJa's commentary on *dary* 'corn'.

ČINGETARĀ

Dmitrieva's 1972 etymology is quite obvious, and it would be wrong to assume any other origin of this word. 'Thin' surely refers to the shape of this plant: millet stalks are much thinner than those of other cerals. They are also more elastic, making millet bend and lie down which makes the impression of thinness even stronger.

KARA TARĀ: name fully clear etymologically and semantically
XŌTARĀ: name unclear

---

32 Perhaps also *tüjtary*.

TARAGAN

FORMS:

taragan **Kmnd.**: Eren 1999 ‖ **Oyr.**: R III 840b ‖ **Tel.**: R III 840b, Eren 1999

taran **Brb.**: R III 841m, ÈSTJa, KWb 380

tarān **Oyr.**: RAltS, Dmitrieva 1972, Brands 1973: 33, ÈSTJa, KWb 380, Eren 1999 ‖ **Tel.**: R III 841m, ÈSTJa, KWb 380, Eren 1999 ‖ **Yak.** Fedotov 1996 ~ *üöre* 'millet; groats'

LANGUAGES:

Brb.: *taran* ‖ **Kmnd.**: *taragan* ‖ **Oyr.**: *taragan, tarān* ‖ **Tel.**: *taragan, tarān* ‖ **Yak.**: *tarān*

ETYMOLOGY:

1935: KWb 380: Brb. *tarian*, Oyr., Tel. *tarān* < Mo.

1960: VGAS: Mo. *tarijan* 'field; sowing', *tarijad* 'sowing; cereal' &c. = OTkc. *taryg* 'crop; cereal'

1973: Brands: 33: < Mo. *tarijan, tarān* 'sowing; cereal'

1974: ÈSTJa: < *tar-a-*; against deriving < Mo. *tarija(n)*

1999: Eren: < Mo.

COMMENTARY:

ÈSTJa is against KWb 380 for phonetic reasons (Mo. *-ija* : Tkc. *-aγa-*), and supports VGAS 62 assuming a parallel evolution *tar-a-* + *-gan* > Tkc. *taragan* &c., Mo. *tarija*. We too, support this conception. Cf. *dary, -tarā*.

TÖGÜ

FORMS:

tögi **MTkc.MK**: (Oghuz.) Eren 1999 'husked millet'

tögü **OTkc.**: TMEN 979, ÈSTJa

töhö **OTkc.**: ÈSTJa

tügä **OTkc.**: VEWT 'husked yellow millet'

tügi **Čag.**: 'husked millet' TMEN 979 ‖ **MTkc.**: VEWT 'husked millet' ‖ **MTkc.MK**: Dankoff/Kelly 1982–85 ‖ **Uyg.**: VEWT 'husked millet'

tügü **MTkc.KD**: نکو 'husked millet'

tui **Trkm.**: طوی ,توی R III 1423b

tüi **Krč.**: Pröhle 1909, VEWT

LANGUAGES:

Čag.: *tügi* ‖ **Krč.**: *tüi* ‖ **MTkc.**: *tügi* ‖ **MTkc.KD**: *tügü* ‖ **MTkc.MK**: *tögi, tügi* ‖ **OTkc.**: *tögü, töhö, tügä* ‖ **Trkm.**: *tui* ‖ **Uyg.**: *tügi*

ETYMOLOGY: see *tüvi* 'rice'

COMMENTARY:

See *tüvi* 'rice'; also *dövme* 'wheat'.

Trkm. *tui* (طوی ,توی, so *tüvi* and *tuvi* can not be excluded either; cf. Trkm. *tüvi* 'rice') is most probably, as suggested by TMEN 979. borrowed from Čag. or another Kipč. source, as is indicated by the voiceless auslaut (cf. also *dary*).

TÜJTARY

FORMS: *tüjtary* Kzk.: TMEN 979 'foxtail millet'

ETYMOLOGY: 1963: TMEN 979: < *tügi-taryg*

COMMENTARY:

The etymology offered by TMEN 979 appears to be quite probable, although the meaning is a little surprising. One could expect such a compound to yield a meaning like 'husked millet' or something similar (cf. *tüvi* 'rice'), not 'foxtail millet'.

While from the semantic point of view a compound *tüj-tary* 'millet with hair' would seem much more likely, and would be a nice parallel to the European names (cf. Eng. *foxtail bristlegrass*, Slav. *włośnica* or Lat. *setaria* (< Lat. *saeta* (*sēta*) '(hard) animal hair, horse hair'; Genaust 1976)), such a solution raises phonetic doubts: in Kzk. 'hair' is called *tük*. Maybe a borrowing from one of the Oghuz. languages?

Though not very probable, it nevertheless cannot be ruled out that *tögü* &c. < *tügī* 'hair' (adj.) < *tük* 'hair' + *-ī* adj. (< Pers.), cf. *tüvi* 'rice'. This idea is interesting semantically but it seems that it, too, leaves the sounding of *tüjtary* unexplained.

ÜGÜR

FORMS:

jögür **MTkc.**: VEWT

jügür **MTkc.MK**: MK III 9 (DTS) || **OTkc.**: Dmitrieva 1972

jügürgün **OTkc.**: Dmitrieva 1972

jügürgün **MTkc.MK**: 'plant similar to millet' Dankoff/Kelly 1982–85

jür **OTkc.**: DTS, Dmitrieva 1972

ögür **MTkc.**: VEWT

öjür **OTkc.**: Egorov 1964, VEWT, Fedotov 1996 'millet; spelt'

ügür **MTkc.MK**: MK I 54, II 121 (DTS), Dankoff/Kelly 1982–85, Eren 1999 s.v. *darı* || **OTkc.**: Dmitrieva 1972

ügürgän **MTkc.MK**: 'grain eaten by Qarluq Turkmān' Dankoff/Kelly 1982–85

üjür **MTkc.MK**: (Oghuz.) Eren 1999 s.v. *darı* || **OTkc.**: DTS, Dmitrieva 1972 || **Uyg.**: Eren 1999 s.v. *darı*

üör **Yak.**: Fedotov 1996 *tarān* ~e 'millet; groats'

ür **OUyg.**: Çevilek 2005

vir **Čuv.**: Nikolьskij 1909, RČuvS-D, RČuvS-E, VEWT, RČuvS-A, Dmitrieva 1972, Eren 1999 s.v. *darı*

LANGUAGES:

Čuv.: *vir* || **MTkc.**: *jögür, jügür, ögür, öjür, ügür* || **MTkc.MK**: *jügür, jügürgün, ügür, ügürgän, üjür* || **OTkc.**: *jügürgün, jür, üjür* || **OUyg.**: *ür* || **Uyg.**: *üjür* || **Yak.**: *üör*

ETYMOLOGY:

1957: Ramstedt: Čuv. *vir* = Mo. *üre* 'seed; fruit'

1964: Egorov: limits himself to a comparison to Mo. *ür* 'grain; seeds; crop'

1972: Dmitrieva: = OTkc. *jügür, jür, ügür, üjür*; indicates a comparison to Kzk. *žügeri* 'corn' and Tat. *öjrä*, Tat. *üre* 'кашица; крупяной суп', Oyr. *üre* 'кашица из толченой крупы', Mo. *ür* 'grain; seeds', OTkc. *jügürgün* 'plant similar to millet'

1995: Stachowski, M.: Khak. *ügrä* 'soup', OUyg. *ügrä* 'gruel; pap' &c. < *ügür-* 'to grate; to squeeze; to grind'

1996: Fedotov: limits himself to indicating a comparison to Mo. *üre* 'seeds; fruit'

1999: Eren s.v. *darı*: *ügür* &c. = Čuv. *vir*

COMMENTARY:

This word has quite a large number of phonetic shapes which is understandable given its phonetical structure. It appears in a relatively large number of meanings, of which only the ones connected with 'millet' have been listed here; see Egorov 1964, Stachowski, M. 1995, Fedotov 1996.

To the best of our knowledge, the only etymology to date is the one proposed by Stachowski, M. 1995: 158. It seems to be based solely on the meanings of the type 'gruel', 'pap', 'soup' and the like, but connecting these two words does not pose any major problems. We know that the Turks have been eating various cereals, including millet, in the form of gruels, mashes and the like (cf. Tryjarski 1993: 120 and others). Shifting the name from 'gruel (or something similar) made of millet' to 'millet' itself is only natural.

However, the morphological structure does pose a problem here. While the 'gruel' &c. words have a vocalic auslaut (Khak. *ügrä* 'soup', OUyg. *ügrä* 'gruel; pap', Tat. *öjrä* 'soup with gruels' &c.), the 'millet' ones have a consonant at the end. In OTkc., the existence of nomen and verbum with the same sounding is not a rare phenomenon, but a unification of meanings 'to grate; to squeeze; to grind' and 'millet' in one stem, with no suffixes, is hardly probable. 'To grind' and 'gruel' would make a more likely couple, but it is the meaning of 'gruel' that has the suffix, and of 'millet' that does not.

It hardly seems plausible that the forms meaning 'gruel' &c. would not be related in this or another way to the words mentioned above but it is impossible to establish the exact nature of this relationship at the moment.

Further bibliography in Eren 1999. Cf. also *öjür* 'wheat', and for the final semantics – *tüvi* 'rice' and *dövme* 'wheat'.

ŽAVERS

FORMS:

žavers (جاورس) **Ott.:** Wiesentahl 1895

žāvers **Ott.:** 'species of millet growing wild among wheat' Redhouse 1921

ETYMOLOGY: as yet not discussed

COMMENTARY:

From Pers. جَاورس žavers ~ گاورس gawres 'foxtail millet (*Setaria italica* P.B.); *Setaria viridis* P.B.'.

On the surface, the semantics might raise doubts here. But setarias, like in all probability other grasses, too, are named in various languages of the world, including those in Asia, with the word for 'millet' and some kind of an adjective (cf. Nowiński

1970: 186), cf. e.g. Russ. *просо венгерское* 'foxtail millet'. This pattern is even reflected in the biological nomenclature: *Setaria italica* P.B. = *Panicum italicum* L. and others, *Setaria viridis* P.B. = *Panicum viride* L.

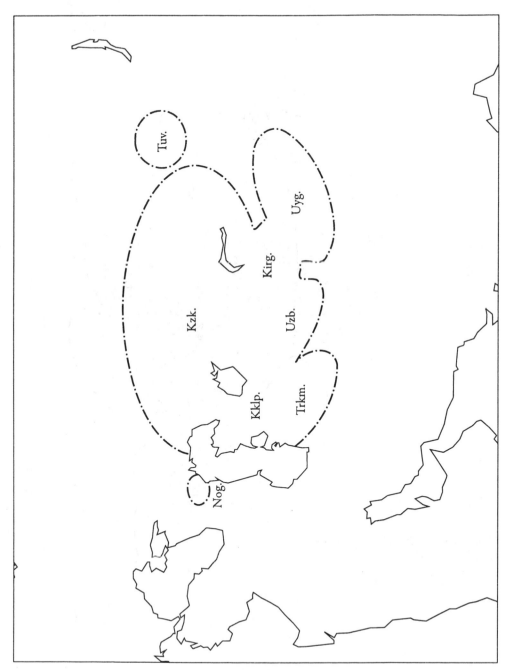

konak 'millet'

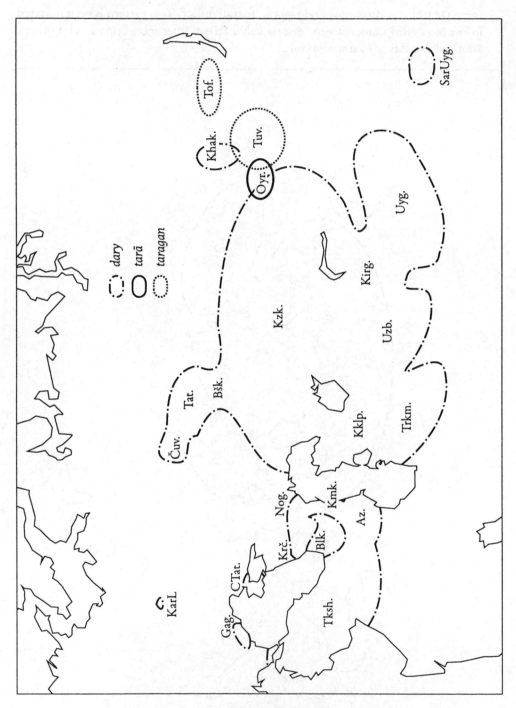

dary 'millet'

In comparison to other cereals, the cultivation of oats began relatively late, only about the beginning of the Common Era. The plant was known much earlier but was regarded as being more of a usable weed, a supplement to wheat or barley. This is most probably the reason why names for 'oats' are so often mixed with names for 'barley' (cf. commentary on *julaf* (point 2), *harva, tay arpasy* 'oats', and *sula* and *arpagan* 'barley').[33] Because the cultivation of oats began so late, it is not entirely clear which region is its homeland. Ancient Greece only knew it as a medicinal weed, the most important cultures of ancient Asia and Africa did not know it as a cereal at all. In China, it appeared in the former role, as late as the 7th c.

It seems the the Tkc. peoples had already known oats in the period before written monuments (cf. commentary on *süle*). Presumably, however, it was not highly regarded, for in ancient texts it is rarely mentioned, unlike e.g. wheat or barley.

The basic name is definitely *süle*. It appears in very many phonetic variants, surprisingly many given its simple sounding. The range of the word *julaf*, the second most common name, is huge, but it is absolutely understandable from a cultural-historical perspective.

FORMS:

arpakan	ovjot	sulū → süle
at tarāzy → a″tarāzy	ovsa	sülü → süle
a″tarāzy	sĕlĕ → süle	suly → süle
bürdük	sinir bozan	sŭly → süle
ebies	sölĕ → süle	sūly → süle
gara gyjak	solo → süle	śĕlĕ → süle
harva	sölö → süle	śĕlĕlli → süle
holo → süle	sōlō → süle	tay-arpasy
hölö → süle	soly → süle	urus arpa
hŭlŭ → süle	sula → süle	uvus
huly → süle	süle	uwys
jolap → julaf	suli → süle	xarva → harva
julaf	süli → süle	zyntxy
nyxa	sully → süle	*žilap → julaf
ovjos	sulu → süle	žylap → julaf

---

33 Interestingly enough, this only concerns oats and barley, not oats and wheat. The only explanation we can offer here is a guess that the Turks have always valued wheat more highly than barley, or that they had known wheat before they learned about barley. The fact that wheat appears in monuments more often seems to support the former rather than the latter. So does *süle* (cf. commentary on *süle*). Concurrently, botanical sources emphasise the antiquity of wheat. However, for how long exactly the Turks have been acquainted with it is unknown.

LANGUAGES:

Az.: *julaf*

Brb.: *soly*

Bšk.: *holo* || *hölö* || *hŭlŭ* || *huly* || *ovsa*

Com.: *sulu*

CTat.: **ʒilap*

Čuv.: *sĕlĕ* || *sölĕ* || *sölö* || *śĕlĕ* || *śĕlĕlli*

Gag.: *julaf*

Kar.: *sülü*

KarC: *julaf* || *ʒylap*

KarT: *uvus*

Khak.: *sula*

Kirg.: *sulu* || *sulŭ* || *suly*

Kklp.: *sully* || *suly*

Kmk.: *nyxa* || *sulu* || *suly*

Koyb.: *sula* || *sulu*

Krč.: *sula*

Krč.Blk.: *zyntxy*

Kyzyl: *sulu*

Kzk.: *sulu* || *suly* || *sūly*

Leb.: *sula*

Nog.: *suly*

Ott.: *julaf* || *sinir bozan*

Oyr.: *sula*

Sag.: *sula* || *sulu*

SarUyg.: *harva* || *xarva*

Šr.: *sula*

Tat.: *julaf* || *solo* || *sölö* || *sōlō* || *soly* || *sŭly*

Tat.dial.: *uwys*

Tat.Gr.: *jolap*

Tel.: *sula*

Tksh.: *julaf*

Tob.: *sulu*

Tof.: *ovjot*

Trkm.: *bürdük* || *gara gyjak* || *ovjos* || *süle* || *süli*

Tuv.: *at tarāzy* || *a"tarāzy* || *sula*

Uyg.: *arpakan* || *sula* || *sulu* || *taɣ-arpasy*

Uzb.: *suli* || *süli* || *urus arpa*

Yak.: *ebies*

ARPAKAN

FORMS: *arpakan* **Uyg.:** R I 334m

ETYMOLOGY: Uyg. form as yet not discussed

COMMENTARY:

The structure of this word is absolutely clear: *arpa* + *-kan*. What seems to be more enigmatic is its meaning, given Tkc. *arpa* 'barley'. However, these two cereals are to some extent unified or mixed by numerous peoples, cf. commentary on *julaf* (point 2), *harva* and *taɣ arpasy*, and *arpagan* 'barley'.

A"TARĀZY

FORMS: *at tarāzy* (*ат тараазы*) **Tuv.:** Dmitrieva 1972: 213 || *a"tarāzy* RTuwS

ETYMOLOGY: 1972: Dmitrieva: < *at* 'horse' + *tarāzy* 'its cereal, grain'

COMMENTARY:

This name is absolutely clear from both morphological and semantic point of view, and it is very difficult to offer an explanation different than the one presented by Dmitrieva 1972.

BÜRDÜK

FORMS: *bürdük* **Trkm.:** R IV 1892m

ETYMOLOGY: see *bordoq* 'roasted corn'

COMMENTARY:

The original meaning of 'grain' is a perfect tertium comparationis for the seemingly unconnected meanings of 'oats' and 'corn'. Cf. *bordoq* 'roasted corn'.

EBIES

FORMS: *ebies* **Yak.**: Slepcov 1964, RJakS, Dmitrieva 1972
ETYMOLOGY:

> 1964: Slepcov 77: < Russ. *ovës* 'oats' with an irregular correspondence *ie* < *jo*, maybe from a dial. pronunciation *ovjes*
>
> 1972: Dmitrieva: < Russ. *ovës* 'oats'
>
> 2003: Anikin: < Russ. *ovës* 'oats'

COMMENTARY:

Dmitrieva 1972 and Anikin 2003 are undoubtedly right, but they entirely disregard the somewhat strange phonetics of the Yak. form, only briefly mentioned by Slepcov 1964 where an unattested Russ.dial. form *ovjes* is proposed. Although there is no proof for this, it seems to be a quite plausible explanation. Another possibility – rather unlikely though, given the cultural realities – would be a graphical borrowing with regressive vocal harmony caused by long (a rendering of the Russ. accent), accented *-ie* in the second syllable (cf. *žesemen* and *žehimien* 'barley').

GARA GYJAK

FORMS: *gara gyjak* **Trkm.**: (Kara-kala) Nikitin/Kerbabaev 1962
ETYMOLOGY: as yet not discussed
COMMENTARY:

GARA:

'Black' is most likely used metaphorically here, meaning 'worse; bad' which is a very common phenomenon in the Tkc. (and other) languages. Such a meaning certainly is derived from the fact that oats were treated as a weed for such a long period.

GYJAK:

Trkm. *gyjak* has a couple of meanings, but the one meant here is definitely 'пырей волосатый; пырей ползучий'.

HARVA

FORMS: *harva* **SarUyg.**: Tenišev 1976 ‖ *xarva* Tenišev 1976
ETYMOLOGY: 1976: Tenišev: ? < *arpa*
COMMENTARY:

The etymology proposed by Tenišev 1976, although presented with a question mark, seems to be very probable. At least, it raises no doubts from the phonetic point of view: for *h-* ~ *x-* cf. SarUyg. *harqa* ~ *xǎřk* 'back' < *arka*, or *horta* 'middle' < *orta* (Tenišev 1976: 29); and for *-rv-*: SarUyg. *terve-* < *terbe-* 'to sway' and others (Tenišev 1976: 27).

What might not be viewed as being absolutely convincing is the semantics (Tkc. *arpa* 'barley'). It must be remembered, however, that these two cereals are mixed to some extent, or unified: cf. *arpa* and the commentary on *julaf* (point 2) and *arpakan*, also *sula* 'barley'. (*H*)*arva* also means 'barley', too.

Steblin-Kamenskij 1982: 36 suggests that Yazg. and OVanj. *xarban* 'millet' is somehow connected with Tkc. *arpa* 'barley', though the SarUyg. form is not listed among the Tkc. words. Due to its initial *x-* ~ *h-*, it is precisely this form that appears to be the closest to the Pamir. words. However, semantics might raise much more serious doubts here, than in the case of a simple comparison of SarUyg. and Tkc. forms.

JULAF

FORMS:

jolap **Tat.Gr.**: Podolsky 1981

julaf **Az.**: RAzS, KTLS, Dmitrieva 1972, 'oats, oats flour' ÈSTJa || **Gag.**: ÈSTJa ||
  KarC: ÈSTJa || **Ott.**: Wiesentahl 1895, Redhouse 1921 || **Tat.**: يولاف R III 555m,
  Tanievъ 1909 || **Tksh.**: KTLS, Dmitrieva 1972

*žilap **CTat.**: Zaatovъ 1906 (in: *žilaply* 'made of oats')

žylap **KarC**: ÈSTJa

LANGUAGES:

Az.: *julaf* || **CTat.**: **žilap* || **Gag.**: *julaf* || **KarC**: *julaf, žylap* || **Ott.**: *julaf* || **Tat.**: *julaf* ||
  Tat.Gr.: *jolap* || **Tksh.**: *julaf*

ETYMOLOGY:

1969: VEWT: only mentions the word, without providing any etymology

1974: ÈSTJa: (?) < Pers. جو *žoŭ* ~ *žav* 'barley', Talyš *žəv-*, dial. *jəv* + Pers. عَلَف [äläf]
       'grass; fodder', Talyš *alaf* 'grass' (< Arab.); so *julaf* < **ju* (< *jəv*) + *alaf* / *ələf* [sic]
       'barley' + 'hay' (< 'grass')

COMMENTARY:

The etymology proposed by ÈSTJa seems a little strange from both phonetic and semantic point of view:

1. We can see no reason, why Pers.dial. *jəv* should render **ju* in Tkc.
2. In the Tkc. languages, noun + noun compounds – such as the one suggested by ÈSTJa – render in the great majority of meanings a material something is made of, or a comparison to something. Therefore, the meaning one should expect from such a form should rather be 'barley grass', 'grass such as barley' and the like. From this point, the road to 'barley' is not long. Particularly in that, as it is noted by ÈSTJa, in many languages including Pers. and Taj., the name for 'barley' evolved into 'oats', or the name for 'oats' originates from the name for 'barley', cf. Klmk. dial. *arva* 'oats' (Tkc. 'barley'), and Ma. *arfa* 'oats; barley'; cf. also *arpakan* and *harva*, also *sula* 'barley'. All this is fairly understandable with regard for the history of oats (see commentary at the beginning of the chapter).

However, none of this information can explain why ÈSTJa assumes a shift from 'grass' to 'hay' on the Tkc. ground.

Deriving *julaf* from a compound of Pers. *žoŭ* ~ *žav* or Pers.dial. *jəv* seems to have an advantage from the point of view of the Tkc. *j-* ~ *ž-* alternation in anlaut but it creates another phonetic obstacle (see above) which we believe is quite serious.

We would like to suggest a slight modification of this etymology, and – as no ulti-mate proof can be presented here – another proposition for explaining this word.

In anlaut, the alternation *j-* ~ *ž-* can be explained by a purely Tkc. alternation which, however, has not been studied thoroughly enough to allow for a full verification of this assumption. However, what seems to be more problematic is the lack of *-v-* and a change from the remaining *-aa-*, *-aə-* &c. into *-u-*. This is why we believe that the first part of this compound should have rather been borrowed from a form such as liter. Pers., i.e. *žoụ*.

The second part definitely should have been a word of back vocal harmony. We could take into consideration such forms as Talyš., Arab. or Pers. (dial., not liter., with non-palatalised short *a*'s). Arab. can probably be excluded, as it would require an assumption, that on the dial. Tkc. ground a presumably local borrowing from dial. Pers. / Talyš was compounded with a borrowing from Arab. which is quite unlikely. On the other hand, a compounding of a form such as the liter. Pers. *žoụ* (which could have appeared in dial., too) with a Pers.dial. / Talyš form [alaf], seems to be quite realistic.

There is still at least one more way of explaining this word. Namely, it could be regarded not as a compound, but as an iotated borrowing form Arab. علف *ʿalaf* 'dry grass; hay; fodder'. Iotation is not a common phenomenon, and definitely not a regular one, which is certainly a weakness of this proposition. Tekin 1975: 205 gives only three examples of modern *ju-* deriving from MTkc. long vowel: *$\bar{i}$-, *$\bar{o}$-, *$\bar{\ddot{o}}$-, and all of them come from SarUyg. As far as our knowledge goes, it has not yet been established what the condi-tions allowing for iotation were in dial. Tksh. (Ott.). If they were the same, one could believe that *ʿa-* was rendered as *$\bar{o}$- > *ju-*[34]. In such a case, only the Arab. form could be taken into consideration, the Pers. *ʿ-* being nothing but a graphical tradition with no importance for the actual sounding.

From the semantic point of view, 'grass; hay; fodder' > 'oats' is at least as probable as 'barley grass' or similar > 'oats', given that oats are often used for fodder.

None of the three propositions is completely convincing. Ultimately, the modified version of ÈSTJa's explanation appears to be the most realistic.

NYXA

FORMS: *nyxa* **Kmk.**: RKmkS, Dmitrieva 1972
ETYMOLOGY: as yet not discussed
COMMENTARY:
The sounding of the word clearly suggests a borrowing, presumably from one of the Cauc. languages, but we have not managed to establish the exact source.

---

34 Although cf. Tksh.dial. *alaf, alef* 'fodder for animals; hay' (Tietze 2000).

OVJOS

FORMS: *ovjos* **Trkm.**: RTrkmS
ETYMOLOGY: as yet not discussed
COMMENTARY:
This word is undoubtedly a borrowing from Russ. *ovjós* id. The initial *o-* supposably indicates that it must have been borrowed from some dial. with an 'okanye' pronunciation, though it would be difficult to confirm this solution, as the Russ. dialectal texts, especially the older ones, do not render the actual sounding precisely. Another possibility would be to assume a partly graphical[35] borrowing. This, however, is definitely less likely from the cultural-historical point of view.

OVJOT

FORMS: *ovjot (овёт)* **Tof.**: RTofS, Stachowski, M. 1999a: 236
ETYMOLOGY: as yet not discussed
COMMENTARY:
This form is undoubtedly a borrowing from Russ. *ovjós* id. The final *-t* is supposably the result of a common but not fully described and not fully predictable alternation *s ~ t*, present in languages of various linguistic families across Siberia, including Tkc. (cf. Stachowski, M. 1999a for further bibliography).

OVSA

FORMS: *ovsa* **Bšk.**: Dmitrieva 1972
ETYMOLOGY: 1972: Dmitrieva: < Russ. *ovës* 'oats'
COMMENTARY:
This form was most probably borrowed from Russ. Gen. in the function of Part. Cf. *prosa* 'millet'.

SINIR BOZAN

FORMS: *sinir bozan* **Ott.**: R IV 696m
ETYMOLOGY: as yet not discussed
COMMENATRY:
This name is unlcear. Maybe it is a substantivised participle in the expression *(birinin) sinirlerini bozmak* 'to annoy'? Such an explanation could be justified by the fact that oats was often regarded as a weed.

---

35 Or even a fully graphical one, if one takes into account that Russ. *ë* is usually printed as *e*.

SÜLE

FORMS:

holo **Bšk.**: Joki 1952, RBškS, KTLS, Dmitrieva 1972, Fedotov 1996

hölö **Bšk.**: Egorov 1964

hŭlŭ **Bšk.**: ÈSTJa

huly **Bšk.**: Joki 1952

sĕlĕ **Čuv.**: Nikolьskij 1909, Ašmarin 1928–50, RČuvS-D, RČuvS-E, Egorov 1964, VEWT, RČuvS-A, ÈSTJa, Fedotov 1996

sölĕ **Čuv.**: VEWT

solo **Tat.**: Voskresenskij 1894, Joki 1952

sölö **Čuv.**: Räsänen 1920 || **Tat.**: سولو R IV 591b, IV 730m, I 1335b, Räsänen 1920, Joki 1952, EWT, ÈSTJa

sōlō **Tat.**: Imanaevъ 1901

soly **Brb.**: ÈSTJa || **Tat.**: RTatS-D, Egorov 1964, KTLS, Dmitrieva 1972, RTatS-G, Fedotov 1996

sula **Khak.**: R IV 772b, RChakS, Egorov 1964, Dmitrieva 1972, ÈSTJa || **Koyb.**: Kannisto 1925: 168, KWb, Fedotov 1996 || **Krč.**: Kannisto 1925: 168 || **Leb.**: Kannisto 1925: 168, Fedotov 1996 || **Oyr.**: R IV 772s, Kannisto 1925: 168, Joki 1952, Egorov 1964, RAltS, VEWT, Dmitrieva 1972, ÈSTJa, KWb, Fedotov 1996 || **Sag.**: Kannisto 1925: 168, Joki 1952, Fedotov 1996 || **Šr.**: R IV 772b, Kannisto 1925: 168, Joki 1952, Fedotov 1996 || **Tel.**: R IV 772b, Räsänen 1920, Kannisto 1925: 168, Joki 1952, 'barley' Ryumina-Sırkaşeva/Kuçigaşeva 1995, Fedotov 1996 || **Tuv.**: RTuwS, Dmitrieva 1972, ÈSTJa || **Uyg.**: Joki 1952

süle **Trkm.**: Joki 1952, Nikitin/Kerbabaev 1962, KTLS, VEWT, Dmitrieva 1972, ÈSTJa

suli **Uzb.**: Joki 1952 'wild oats (*Avena fatua*)', RUzbS-A, Egorov 1964, VEWT, Dmitrieva 1972, ÈSTJa, RUzbS-Š

süli **Trkm.**: Alijiv/Böörijif 1929 || **Uzb.** KTLS

sully **Kklp.**: RKklpS-BB, Dmitrieva 1972

sulu **Com.**: R IV 775b, Joki 1952, KWb, Fedotov 1996 || **Kirg.**: R IV 775b, RKirgS-Ju44, RKirgS-Ju57, Egorov 1964, KTLS, Dmitrieva 1972, ÈSTJa, Fedotov 1996 || **Kmk.**: RKmkS, Egorov 1964, Dmitrieva 1972, ÈSTJa || **Koyb.**: Joki 1952 || **Kyzyl**: Joki 1952, ÈSTJa || **Kzk.**: R IV 775b, Räsänen 1920, Joki 1952, VEWT, KWb || **Sag.**: Joki 1952 || **Tob.**: Joki 1952 || **Uyg.**: سۇلۇ RUjgS, KTLS, Joki 1952, Egorov 1964, ÈSTJa

sulū **Kirg.**: Joki 1952

sülü **Kar.**: ÈSTJa

suly **Kirg.**: Mašanovъ 1899 || **Kklp.**: RKklpS-ST, Egorov 1964, RKklpS-B, ÈSTJa || **Kmk.**: ÈSTJa || **Kzk.**: KTLS, Egorov 1964, Dmitrieva 1972, ÈSTJa, DFKzk, DKzkF || **Nog.**: RNogS, Dmitrieva 1972, ÈSTJa

sŭly **Tat.**: ÈSTJa

sūly **Kzk.**: RKzkS-46, RKzkS-54

śĕlĕ **Čuv.**: Dmitrieva 1972

śĕlĕlli **Čuv.**: Dmitrieva 1972

LANGUAGES:

Brb.: *soly* || **Bšk.**: *holo, hölö, hŭlŭ, huly* || **Com.**: *sulu* || **Čuv.**: *sĕlĕ, sölö, sölö, śĕlĕ, śĕlĕlli* ||
Kar.: *sülü* || **Khak.**: *sula* || **Kirg.**: *sulu, sulū, suly* || **Kklp.**: *sully, suly* || **Kmk.**: *sulu, suly* ||
Koyb.: *sula, sulu* || **Krč.**: *sula* || **Kyzyl**: *sulu* || **Kzk.**: *sulu, suly, sūly* || **Leb.**: *sula* || **Nog.**:
suly || **Oyr.**: *sula* || **Sag.**: *sula, sulu* || **Šr.**: *sula* || **Tat.**: *solo, sölö, sōlō, soly, sŭly* || **Tel.**: *sula* ||
Tob.: *sulu* || **Trkm.**: *süle, süli* || **Tuv.**: *sula* || **Uyg.**: *sula, sulu* || **Uzb.**: *suli, süli*

ETYMOLOGY:

1920: Räsänen: ~ Mo. *suli*

1952: Joki: ~ or rather < Mo. *suli* &c.; Uzb. *suli* 'common wild oat (*Avena fatua*)',
Trkm. *süle* < Mo.; Čuv. = or < Tat.
further etymology unclear; maybe a common PAlt. name

1969: VEWT: Čuv. *sĕlĕ, sölĕ* < Tat. *sölö*; Trkm. *süle*, Uzb. *suli* < Mo. *suli*

1972: Clauson: < *suv* 'water'

1974: ÈSTJa: limits himself to summarizing and commenting previous propositions:
against Clauson 1972 and Dmitrieva TÈ 97–8 (quoted after ÈSTJa), who < *suv*
'water' + *-lu* (phonetics)

1976: KWb: expression unclear; perhaps = Mo. *suli* &c.

COMMENTARY:

This word is also common in the Mo. languages, usually meaning various wild species
of grass. As it is supposed by Joki 1952, this is most probably the original meaning,
which is understandable since oats were for a long time considered to be a weed, and its
cultivation only began at the beginning of the Common Era; cf. also Genaust 1976.

The proposition of Clauson 1972 and Dmitrieva TÈ 97–8 (quoted after ÈSTJa)
is, as it is noted by ÈSTJa, deeply problematic for phonetic reasons (cf. Khak., Tuv.
sula, Uyg. *sulu*, Uzb. *suli* instead of expected **suvluk*, **suglug* if they were to come
from **sug/vlug*). Dmitrieva's attempt at explaining the semantics by stating that
oats are a fodder liked by horses, and that they salivate when eating it (for 'water' >
'saliva' cf. Tksh. *ağız suyu* and others), is even more problematic than ÈSTJa rates
it. However, it needs to be noted in defence of this proposition, that Khak., Tuv.,
Uyg. and Uzb. forms could actually be borrowed from other Tkc. or Mo. languages.
Still, this would by no means solve the difficulties with the semantics. For more on
the phonetics cf. below.

Unfortunately, to date this is the only full etymology that has been presented. Joki's
1952 suggestion that the word might originate from the times of the PAlt. union[36] appears
to be very pertinent but does not in fact explain anything. It merely moves the question
back in time. We cannot, however, offer a more exhaustive explanation, either.

We believe that the original form of our word should have sounded **solo*, and
even this statement can we only support by guesses: 1. the Mo. forms indicate a front
vocalism; the fluctuations in Tkc. are apparently the result of the as yet undescribed
alternation front ~ back vocalism; 2. it is rather improbable that the *u* in the first

---

36 Or at least from the period of close contacts between the Tkc. and Mo. languages, i.e. of areal
union, were a genetic relationship to never have existed.

syllable should > *o*; **3.** we believe that the evolution **solo* > *sola, sula* > *suly, sulu, süle* is more natural for the Tkc. languages than any other, which would have to be assumed for a different set of original vowels.

This reconstruction does not explain all of the Tkc. forms. What the source of long vowels in Kirg. *sulū* and Kzk. *sūly* is, we do not know.

The diffusion of this word in the Alt. languages and a very high number of phonetic variants, especially high for a word of such a simple structure, indicates that it must be old, perhaps as old as PAlt. Cf. also footnote 23.

For borrowings from Tkc. to other languages see bibliography in ÈSTa and Kannisto 1925.

TAΓ-ARPASY

FORMS: *taɣ-arpasy* **Uyg.:** تاغ ارپاسی Raquette 1927
ETYMOLOGY: as yet not discussed
COMMENTARY:

Being absolutely clear morphologically (lit. 'mountain barley'), this name is utterly obscure semantically.

The Uyg. word *taɣ* – which is perhaps closely related to Kzk. *tak-tak* 'barley' (unclear, too) – has two meanings: 'mountain' and 'odd (number)'. It would be difficult to assume, that the one in question is the latter, but it is also quite impossible to explain why the Uyghurs should call 'oats' a 'mountain barley'. Climatic requirements of oats are much higher than those of barley; in the mountains it does not grow above 2000 m above sea level while barley sets the world record in this regard, growing as high as 4646 m above sea level in Tibet (Nowiński 1970: 182).

The second part of this compound could be regarded as another example of a very common unification/mixing of oats and barley (cf. commentary on *julaf* (point 2) and *arpakan*, also *sula* 'barley'), though the existence of Uyg. *arpa* 'barley' seems to speak against it.

Maybe then *taɣ* (presumably, etymologically different from Tkc. *tag* 'mountain') has originally had a meaning of 'wild' or something similar, a trace of which would be a modern 'odd (number)'? This, given that oats were held in low esteem, could explain such a compound as Uyg. *taɣ-arpasy* but would be useless if not preventing in the case of Kzk. *tak-tak* 'barley', in light of the strange structure of the latter. Unless, of course, the two words turned out not to be related in any way after all.

URUS ARPA

FORMS: *urus arpa* **Uzb.:** Smolenskij 1912
ETYMOLOGY: as yet not discussed
COMMENTARY:

Urus does not appear in modern Uzb. dictionaries (UzbRS, Maъrufov 1981). We believe, however, that it is just a better assimilated version of the modern word *rus* 'Russian[37]. The name would then mean liter. 'Russian barley'. This would suggest that the Uzbeks knew barley before they learned about oats from the Russians, or that oats was the basic cereal grown by the Russians living in Uzbekistan, while the Uzbeks mainly cultivated barley. The former of these two possibilities seems to be the more plausible, but one does not really exclude the other.

UVUS

FORMS: *uvus ywyc* אובוס **KarT:** R I 1787m
ETYMOLOGY: 1893: Radloff: < Russ. *ovёsъ* 'oats'
COMMENTARY:

The etymology proposed by Radloff 1893–1911 appears to be correct, although 1. another Slav. language cannot be excluded (cf. Pol. *owies* || Ukr. *oves*); 2. it completely omits the question of the unusual vocalism in Kar. Unfortunately, we cannot explain it in a fully convincing way, either.

We believe that the vocalism indicates that the word was not borrowed to Kar. directly from Russ., but via MTat.

There exists another, though less likely, possibility of a double mistake (copyist's? printer's? Radloff's?) and reading? writing? ן instead of ו, i.e. *uvus* instead of *ovos*, which would be a much more understandable form, and really pointing to Russ. as the source of the borrowing. However, it still requires the assumption of a double mistake in a five-letter word.

UWYS

FORMS: *uwys* **Tat.dial.:** Adjagaši 2005: 153
ETYMOLOGY: 2005: Adjagaši: < MTat. **ovus* < ORuss. / Russ.N.dial. [ovós]
COMMENTARY:

We can see no reason to cast doubt upon Adjagaši's 2005: 153 etymology. Cf. *uvus*.

ZYNTXY

FORMS: *zyntxy* **Krč.Blk.:** RKrčBlkS, Dmitrieva 1972
ETYMOLOGY: as yet not discussed
COMMENTARY:

The sounding of this word suggests a borrowing, presumably from one of the Cauc. languages. Unfortunately, we have not managed to establish the exact source.

---

37 In such a case, a double borrowing of *rus* would need to be assumed. An earlier one, when Russ. was not yet so widely known by the Uzbeks, and a later one, when it was already the mother tongue for many of them. Or alternately, that the sounding was corrected some time after the borrowing.
It cannot be excluded either, that *urus* is nothing but the real Uzb. sounding, while *rus* corresponds faithfully to the Russ. orthography.
As a matter of fact, all these possibilities seem to be reasonably plausible.

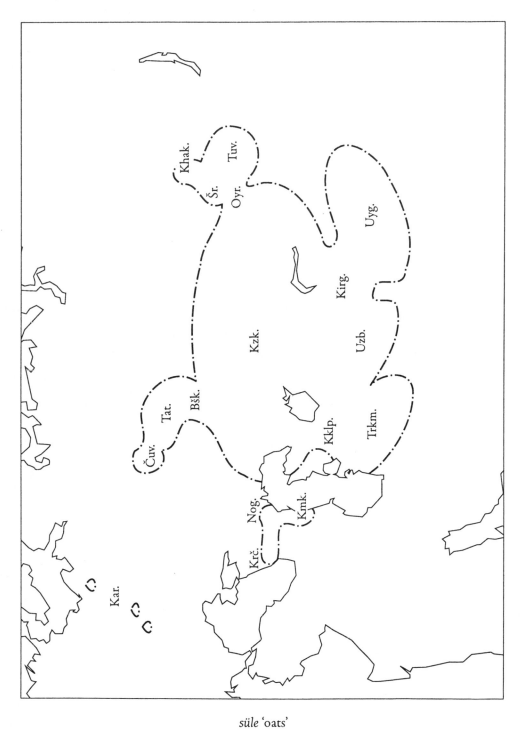

süle 'oats'

RICE

ORYZA SATIVA L.

Rice is one of the most important cultivated plants in the world. It originates from the Indian and SE Asian centres. In India, where it had probably been domesticated, it was already known in the 2nd millennium BC; it spread to China about three thousand years BC (in year 2700 BC it had already been one of the five most important plants sown by emperor Chen-Nung himself during the vernal equinox). It was brought relatively late to Persia, but must have already been known there in the 4th c. BC when the Greeks learned about it from the Persians (see *pirinč*). It then spread to Syria, and later to Egypt (brought by the Arabs in the 8th c.). In the 15th c., the Portuguese took it to the western coast of Africa, and the Arabs to the Eastern. By 1493 it had already reached America thanks to Spaniards.

Nowadays, there exist more then ten thousand varieties of rice, 800 in India alone. It is the most basic source of nourishment in many countries, especially in the Far East (Nowiński 1970: 202–3).

Given the above information, it might be surprising that none of the names for 'rice' in the Tkc. languages is of Chin. origin. It seems scarcely possible that such a borrowing would never have occurred. We probably should presume that this word (or words?) was later displaced by borrowings from other languages (of higher prestige?) and native names (more understandable, like *akbydā* or *döge*).

FORMS:

ak bydā → akbydā	dögö → tüvi	gürünž → gürüč
akbydā	dŏgŏ → tüvi	gürüž → gürüč
ak h(ü)rüpē	döğü → tüvi	irīs → ris
aryš	dügi → tüvi	küriš → gürüč
birinž → pirinč	dugu → tüvi	kürüč → gürüč
biriňč → pirinč	dügü → tüvi	kürüš → gürüč
bryndz → pirinč	düğü → tüvi	pirinč
bürinč → pirinč	düjü → tüvi	pirinž → pirinč
bürünč → pirinč	erz	prinč → pirinč
? buryž → pirinč	görbč → gürüč	ris → ris
čeltik	görič → gürüč	risa → ris
čeltik pirinži → čeltik ‖ pirinč	gurinž → gürüč	risъ → ris
čeltuk → čeltik	guriš → gürüč	saly → šaly
čeltük → čeltik	güriš → gürüč	šal → šaly
čeltūk arpasy → čeltik	guruč → gürüč	šaly
čiltik → čeltik	gürüč	šāly → šaly
döge → tüvi	gürünč → gürüč	šeltūk → čeltik

šoli → šaly
tögi → tüvi
tok(u)rak

tügi → tüvi
tuturgan
tuturgu → tuturgan

tuturkan → tuturgan

LANGUAGES:

Az.: *dügü* || *düjü*
Bšk.: *dögö* || *risa*
Com.: *tuturgan*
CTat.: *princ*
Čag.: *čeltük* || *tuturgu*
Čuv.: *ris* || *risƅ*
Gag.: *pirinč*
KarC: *princ*
KarH: *bryndz*
KarT: *biriňč*
Khak.: *ris*
Khal.: *biriňž* || *dügi*
Kirg.: *kürüč* || *kürüš* || *šaly*
Kklp.: *guriš* || *güriš* || *šaly*
Kmk.: *dugu* || *dügü*
Krč.Blk.: *princ*

Kzk.: *küriš* || *saly* || *šaly*
MTkc.: *gurinž*
MTkc.H: *tuturgan*
MTkc.IM: *tuturgan*
MTkc.KD: *tuturkan*
MTkc.MA.B: *tok(u)rak* ||
  tokurgak
MTkc.MK: *tuturkan*
Nog.: *buryž* || *dügi*
OTkc.: *görbč* || *gürüč* ||
  gürünč || *tögi* || *tuturkan*
Ott.: *čeltik* || *čeltik pirinži*
  || *čeltuk* || *čeltük arpasy*
  || *čiltik* || *erz* || *pirinč* ||
  pirinž || *šeltük*
Oyr.: *ris*

Tat.: *aryš* || *čeltik* || *döge* ||
  dögö || *dǒgǒ* || *kürüš*
Tksh.: *pirinč*
Tksh.dial.: *döǧü* || *düǧü*
Tof.: *ak h(ü)rüpē*
Trkm.: *bürinč* || *bürünč* ||
  šaly || *šāly* || *tüvi*
Tuv.: *ak bydā* || *akbydā* || *ris*
Uyg.: *görbč* || *gürüč* ||
  gürünž || *gürüž* || *šal* ||
  tügi
Uzb.: *birinž* || *görič* || *guruč*
  || *gürünč* || *šaly* || *šoli*
Yak.: *irīs* || *ris*

AKBYDĀ

FORMS: *ak bydā* **Tuv.:** Dmitrieva 1972 || *akbydā* RTuwS
ETYMOLOGY: 1972: Dmitrieva: < *ak* 'white' + *bydā* 'gruel'
COMMENTARY:

This name is absolutely clear morphologically: Tkc. *ak* 'white' + Tkc. *bugdaj* 'wheat'. The absence of *bydā* in Tuv. does not appear to be a serious argument against such an explanation. However, the short -*y*- might be surprising in the light of the original -*ug*-. It is possible, though, that this is only a spurious incompatibility: 1. the length of vowels in non-first syllables is marked in an irregular manner in Tuv.; 2. it could have been shortened secondarily, resulting from the proximity of another long vowel.

AK H(Ü)RÜPĒ

FORMS: *ak h(ü)rüpē* **Tof.:** RTofS
ETYMOLOGY:
   1971: Rassadin: *hürpē* < Russ. *krupa* 'gruel'
   1995: Buraev: *h(ü)rüpē* < Russ. *krupa* 'gruel'
COMMENTARY:

This name is absolutely clear. We can see no reasons to assume a metaphorical use of *ak* here. The shift from 'gruel' to 'rice' is obvious, given the most popular method of preparation.

ARYŠ

FORMS: *aryš* Tat.: Voskresenskij 1894

COMMENTARY: as yet not discussed in the meaning of 'rice'

ETYMOLOGY:

Aryš is a common name for 'rye' in the Tkc. languages. We know of no other word that has both these two meanings simultaneously. Perhaps, the similarity of sounding to Russ. *ris* was of some significance here; at any rate a separate/repeated borrowing must be ruled out as then the prothesis could not be expected to sound **a-*: it would have to be at least **y-* or more probably **i-(ris)* (cf. *aryš* 'rye'). Perhaps then a contamination?

ČELTIK

FORMS:

čeltik Ott.: چلتیك 'unhusked rice and others' R III 1980m, 'rice field' Wiesentahl 1895; چلتك, لتیـك 'rice field; rice on the field; unhusked rice' Redhouse 1921 ‖ Tat.: چلتك Tanievъ 1909

čeltik pirinǯi Ott.: (چلتك برنجی) 'unhusked rice' Redhouse 1921

čeltuk Ott.: چلتوك 'provincial for چلتیك' Redhouse 1921

čeltük Čag.: چلتوك id. R III 1980m

čeltük arpasy Ott.: Tietze 2002– s.v. çeltik

čiltik Ott.: چیلتیك 'rice on the field' R III 2139m

šeltük Ott.: شلتوك vulg. چلتیك 'rice field; rice on the field' Redhouse 1921

LANGUAGES:

Čag.: *čeltük* ‖ Ott.: *čeltik, čeltik pirinǯi, čeltuk, čeltük arpasy, čiltik, šeltük* ‖ Tat.: *čeltik*

ETYMOLOGY:

1999: Eren: < Pers. *šaltūk* 'unhusked rice'; for Pers. *š-* > Tksh. *č-* cf. Tksh. *čakal*

2002: Tietze: < Pers. *šaltūk* 'unhusked rice'; for Pers. *š-* > Tksh. *č-* cf. Tksh. *čorba*

COMMENTARY:

We can see no reason to doubt Eren's 1999 proposition. A few details, however, remain to be explained. The Pers. form has a different anlaut and vocalism than the Tkc. ones. Presumably, the change in the anlaut happened during or very shortly after the borrowing since there are no *š-* forms in Tkc.[38] As for the vowels, we have two contradictory hints:

1. Ott. *čeltük arpasy* indicates that the front harmony of the Tkc. forms results from the infuence of palatal *č-*, and a secondary 'reharmonization' of the whole word: Pers. *šaltūk* > ? Ott. ? Pre-Ott. **čaltuk* > *čeltuk* > *čeltük* > *čeltik* or *čeltuk* > *čeltük, čeltik*. This route is also pointed to by Tksh.dial. *čeltük*.

2. Russ. *čaltyk* 'čeltik', due to the initial *č-* should be considered a borrowing from Tkc. rather than Pers.[39] In such case, however, the following chain of changes should be

---

38 Though not attested, in theory a MPers. **č-* form could be assumed, too, as it would still yield *š* in NPers.; cf. e.g. Maciuszak 2003: 94.

39 Also Vasmer 1959, even if without giving a reason, derives the Russ. word from Tksh. or Az.

assumed: Pers. *šaltūk* > ? Ott. ? Pre-Ott. **čaltuk* > **čaltyk* > **čeltik*. This solution, as opposed to 1., gives no convenient base for explaining *čeltük*.

Perhaps the only way to reconcile these two arguments, is to assume different evolutions of our word in Tksh. dialects (possibly, resulting from repeated, independent borrowings) which, however, finally yielded a single sounding.

ERZ

FORMS: *erz* (ارز) **Ott.**: Wiesentahl 1895, *erz* Redhouse 1921
ETYMOLOGY: as yet not discussed
COMMENTARY:

This name is unclear. The sounding seems to point to Gr., but the Gr. form is ὄριζον, ὄριζα (Woodhouse 1910). Perhaps from a dialectal form or from an oblique case?

GÜRÜNČ

FORMS:
görič **Uzb.**: VEWT
görȫč **OTkc.**: VEWT ‖ **Uyg.**: Menges 1933
gurinž **MTkc.MA.B**: Borovkov 1971: 102
guriš **Kklp.**: RKklpS-BB, Dmitrieva 1972
güriš **Kklp.**: RKklpS-ST, RKklpS-B
guruč **Uzb.**: ('husked') RUzbS-A, (no description) RUzbS-A, Dmitrieva 1972
gürüč **OTkc.**: VEWT, Dmitrieva 1972 ‖ **Uyg.**: كورج RUjgS
gürünč **OTkc.**: Dmitrieva 1972 ‖ **Uzb.**: (كرج) Nalivkinъ 1895
gürünž **Uyg.**: كورنج Raquette 1927
gürüž **Uyg.**: كورنج Raquette 1927 ‖ **Uzb.**: 'gruel' Lapin 1899, Smolenskij 1912
küriš **Kzk.**: RKzkS-46, RKzkS-54, Dmitrieva 1972, DFKzk
kürüč **Kirg.**: 'husked rice' RKirgS-Ju44, RKirgS-Ju57, VEWT, Dmitrieva 1972
kürüš **Kirg.**: Mašanovъ 1899, Katanovъ 1909 ‖ **Tat.**: VEWT
LANGUAGES:
Kirg.: *kürüč, kürüš* ‖ **Kklp.**: *guriš, güriš* ‖ **Kzk.**: *küriš* ‖ **MTkc.**: *gurinž* ‖ **OTkc.**: *görȫč, gürüč, gürünč* ‖ **Tat.**: *kürüš* ‖ **Uyg.**: *görȫč, gürüč, gürünž, gürüž* ‖ **Uzb.**: *görič, guruč, gürünč*
ETYMOLOGY:
1969: VEWT: considers *gürünč* to be the same word as MTkc. *küršek* 'millet boiled in water or milk with butter' and, (with a question mark) Krč. *gyrsyn* 'bread' (? Čuv. > **kürźε* > Fi. *kyrsä* 'bread')
1972: Dmitrieva: Kirg. *kürüč*, Kklp. *guriš*, Kzk. *küriš*, OTkc. *gürü(n)č*, Uzb. *guruč* < Ir. *gürünč* 'rice'
COMMENTARY:

The etymology offered by Dmitrieva 1972 may well be true, although it does raise some phonetic doubts. As for the Ir. etymon, the shape *gurinž* seems to be much more realistic (Hübschmann 1897: 27). This word was presumably borrowed at least a couple of times, as is indicated by the different assimilations of the vowels (*u-u*, *ü-ü*, *ü-i* and the incomprehensible forms with *ö*[40] and Kklp. *u-i*) and consonants (*g-(n)č*, *g-(n)ǯ*, *g-š*, *k-č*, *k-š*) but the exact routes of its penetration[41] are impossible to reconstruct, not at least within the current state of the subject of historical phonetics of individual Tkc. languages.

The comparison to MTkc. *kuršek* proposed by VEWT seems realistic phonetically, but a little odd on the semantic side. To the best of our knowledge, there are no parallels for one word having the meanings of 'rice' and 'millet' at the same time.[42]

Cf. *pirinč*.

PIRINČ

FORMS:

birinǯ **Khal.**: Doerfer 1987 ‖ **Uzb.**: 'groats' Lapin 1899, Smolenskij 1912
birińč **KarT**: KRPS
bryndz **KarH**: KRPS
bürinč **Trkm.**: Alijiv/Böörijif 1929
bürünč **Trkm.**: RTrkmS, Dmitrieva 1972
? *buryž* **Nog.**: RNogS, Dmitrieva 1972
čeltik pirinǯi **Ott.**: (جلنك برجى) 'unhusked rice' Redhouse 1921
pirinč **Gag.**: Dmitrieva 1972 ‖ **Ott.**: (پرنج) Wiesentahl 1895 ‖ **Tksh.**: Dmitrieva 1972
pirinǯ **Ott.**: Redhouse 1921
prinč **CTat.**: Zaatovъ 1906 ‖ **KarC**: Levi 1996 ‖ **Krč.Blk.**: RKrčBlkS, Dmitrieva 1972

LANGUAGES:

CTat.: *prinč* ‖ **Gag.**: *pirinč* ‖ **KarC.**: *prinč* ‖ **KarH.**: *bryndz* ‖ **KarT.**: *birińč* ‖ **Khal.**: *birinǯ* ‖ **Krč.Blk.**: *prinč* ‖ **Nog.**: *buryž* ‖ **Ott.**: *čeltik pirinǯi, pirinč, pirinǯ* ‖ **Tksh.**: *pirinč* ‖ **Trkm.**: *bürinč, bürünč* ‖ **Uzb.**: *birinǯ*

ETYMOLOGY:

1972: Dmitrieva: Gag. *pirinč*, Krč.Blk. *prinč*, Nog. *buryž*, Trkm. *bürünč*, Tksh. *pirinč* < Ir. *pirinč* 'rice; латунь'[43]

1999: Eren: < Pers. *birinǯ*

COMMENTARY:

Dmitrieva's 1972 proposition seems very plausible. We can only add, that Pers. *birinǯ* ~ *gurinǯ* < Skr. *vrīhī* or Afgh. *vriže* (Laufer 1919: 393). Laufer also believes that reconstructing Av. **verenǯa* (Horn 1893: 208) or Ir. **vrinǯi-? *vriži-?* (Hübschmann 1897: 27) is wrong for historical reasons: according to his sources, rice only gained

---

40 The evolution *ö* > *ü* is natural in the Tkc. languages; the opposite is not.

41 At least some of the forms were probably borrowed with the mediation of another Tkc. language.

42 *Tüvi* &c. 'rice' = *tögü* 'millet' is an exception here. However, in this example the differentiation of the semantics results from the source of this word: **tög-* 'to beat, to hit', being absolutely neutral with regard to species.

43 The missing "<" sign in Dmitrieva 1972: 216 is perhaps a typographical error.

popularity in Persia after the Arabic conquest. However, this does not exclude the possibility that the Pers. could have known rice earlier. According to Nowiński 1970: 203, it is from Pers. that the Greeks became acquainted with rice during the invasion of Alexander the Great. Given the above, we believe, even if we cannot prove it, that at least Av. **verenža* might well have existed: if the Pers. had already known rice in the 4th c. BC (and it is much more probable that they would have learned about it from India rather than China at this time), and its modern name is of Indian origin, too, we suppose that the word may well be an old borrowing in Pers., perhaps even from before the 4th c. BC, and therefore that it probably had existed in Av. as well.

Cf. *gürünč*.

RIS

FORMS:

irīs Yak.: Slepcov 1975 (od 1925)

ris Čuv.: RČuvS-D, RČuvS-E, RČuvS-A, Dmitrieva 1972 ‖ **Khak.**: RChakS, Dmitrieva 1972 ‖ **Oyr.**: RAltS, Dmitrieva 1972 ‖ **Tuv.**: RTuwS, Dmitrieva 1972 ‖ **Yak.**: RJakS, Dmitrieva 1972, Slepcov 1975 (od 1925)

risa Bšk.: Dmitrieva 1972

risъ Čuv.: Nikolьskij 1909

LANGUAGES:

Bšk.: *risa* ‖ **Čuv.**: *ris, risъ* ‖ **Khak.**: *ris* ‖ **Oyr.**: *ris* ‖ **Tuv.**: *ris* ‖ **Yak.**: *irīs, ris*

ETYMOLOGY:

1972: Dmitrieva: Čuv., Khak., Oyr., Tuv., Yak. *ris* < Russ. *ris*, and points to a comparison with OInd. *vrīhis* 'rice' (after: Vasmer 1986–87)

COMMENTARY:

It is difficult to find fault with the etymology proposed by Dmitrieva 1972.

ŠALY

FORMS:

saly Kklp.: RKklpS-B, RKklpS-ST, Dmitrieva 1972 ‖ **Kzk.**: 'unhusked' DFKzk

šal Uyg.: شال RUjgS; Raquette 1927 'rice on field', Jarring 1998: 14 'rice; rice as a plant; rice on field; unhusked rice'

šaly Kirg.: 'unhusked, rice as a plant' RKirgS-Ju44, RKirgS-Ju57, (no commentary) Dmitrieva 1972 ‖ **Kzk.**: 'unhusked rice' DFKzk ‖ **Trkm.**: Nikitin/Kerbabaev 1962 ‖ **Uzb.**: 'plant' (شالی) Nalivkinъ 1895, Lapin 1899, Smolenskij 1912

šāly Trkm.: Alijiv/Böörijif 1929

šoli Uzb.: ('unhusked') RUzbS-A, (no description) RUzbS-Š, ('unhusked') Dmitrieva 1972

LANGUAGES:

Kirg.: *šaly* ‖ **Kklp.**: *saly* ‖ **Kzk.**: *saly, šaly* ‖ **Trkm.**: *šaly, šāly* ‖ **Uyg.**: *šal* ‖ **Uzb.**: *šaly, šoli*

ETYMOLOGY:

1972: Dmitrieva: only points to a comparison with Mo. *sali*

1998: Jarring: 14: < Pers. *šālī* 'unhusked rice'

COMMENTARY:

We can see no reason to discard the etymology proposed by Jarring 1998: 14. We would only remark that *-i* was probably understood as a Px in Uyg., and hence the form *šal*.

TOKURGAK

FORMS:

tok(u)rak **MTkc.MA.B**: Borovkov 1971 'rice for pilaff'

tokurgak **MTkc.MA.B**: Borovkov 1971: 108

ETYMOLOGY: as yet not discussed

COMMENTARY:

The etymology of this word is not clear. We believe that it is a morphologically adapted (folk etymology) version of *tuturgan* (probably < Mo., cf.) associated with *tok-* 'to knock, to tap, to hit' (for semantics cf. *tüvi*, also *dövme* 'wheat') and with a Tkc. suffix *-ak*. The suffix *-gan* is there in the Tkc. languages, too, so here an adaptation would not be necessary. However, if the meaning was to be similar to 'beaten (out)', *-ak* would seem to suit it better.

Cf. *tuturgan*.

TUTURGAN

FORMS:

tuturgan **Com.**: R III 1484m || **MTkc.H**: طوطورغان || **MTkc.IM**

tuturgu **Čag.**: توتورغو R III 1484m

tuturkan **OTkc.**: Dmitrieva 1972 || **MTkc.KD**: نترقان || **MTkc.MK**: Ligeti 1951–52: 87

LANGUAGES:

Com.: *tuturgan* || **Čag.**: *tuturgu* || **MTkc.H**: *tuturgan* || **MTkc.IM**: *tuturgan* || **MTkc.KD**: *tuturkan* || **MTkc.MK**: *tuturkan* || **OTkc.**: *tuturkan*

ETYMOLOGY:

1951: Ligeti: 87: < Mo. *tuturyan* id.

1963: TMEN: limits itself to scepticism towards Ligeti: '[...] hier dürfte der strikte Nachweis Mo. Herkunft allerdings schwerig sein' (TMEN I: 5)

1972: Dmitrieva: only points to the comparison with WMo

COMMENTARY:

This word is not wholly comprehensible. Its Mo. origin, as proposed by Ligeti 1951–52: 87, is possible but to the best of our knowledge, the word remains equally unclear on the Mo. ground. This could suggest that the opposite direction of borrowing is no less probable. However, were our proposition of explaining *tokurgak* to prove true, it would point to the direction proposed by Ligeti. Finally, the word could have been borrowed to Mo. and Tkc. from yet another language independently.

Not knowing the eventual etymology of our word, we cannot determine whether the final *-gan* is a native Mo. (Tkc.?) suffix, or a morphologically (phonetically?) adapted part of a foreign etymon.

Cf. *tokurgak.*

TÜVI

FORMS:

döge **Tat.**: RTatS-D, TMEN 979, RTatS-G, Dmitrieva 1972

dögö **Bšk.**: RBškS, TMEN 979, Dmitrieva 1972, Eren 1999 || **Tat.**: Voskresenskij 1894

dŏgŏ **Tat.**: VEWT, TMEN 979

döğü **Tksh.dial.**: 'fine groats' Eren 1999

dügi **Khal.**: Doerfer 1987 || **Nog.**: RNogS, TMEN 979, Dmitrieva 1972, Eren 1999

dugu **Kmk.**: Németh 1911/12, VEWT

dügü **Az.**: R III 1802m, VEWT. TMEN 979 || **Kmk.**: Németh 1911/12, TMEN 979, RKmkS, Dmitrieva 1972

düğü **Tksh.dial.**: 'fine groats' Eren 1999

düjü **Az.**: RAzS, TMEN 979, Dmitrieva 1972

tögi **OTkc.**: Erdal 340 'husked and/or ground cereal'

tügi **Uyg.**: 'husked rice' R III 1539m, VEWT

tüvi **Trkm.**: Alijiv/Böörijif 1929, RTrkmS, VEWT, TMEN 979, Dmitrieva 1972, Eren 1999 'rice; pilaff'

LANGUAGES:

Az.: *dügü, düjü* || **Bšk.**: *dögö* || **Khal.**: *dügi* || **Kmk.**: *dugu, dügü* || **Nog.**: *dügi* || **OTkc.**: *tögi* || **Tat.**: *döge, dögö, dŏgŏ* || **Tksh.dial.**: *döğü, düğü* || **Trkm.**: *tüvi* || **Uyg.**: *tügi*

ETYMOLOGY:

1963: TMEN: **tügi*

1969: VEWT: limits itself to enumerating the forms

1974: ÈSTJa s.v. *dary*: OTkc. *tögü, töhö* probably do not belong to the same group as *dary*

1991: Erdal: 340: OTkc. *tögi* 'husked and/or ground cereal' < *tög* 'to grind; to crush'

2004: Pomorska: 120: supports Erdal 1991: 340

COMMENTARY:

This word is quite common in the Tkc. languages, and is found in two basic meanings: '(husked) rice' (more common) and 'millet' (less common)'.

It seems that TMEN's 979 reconstruction of **tügi* might perhaps need a modification of the first vowel: **ö* seems to be much more probable for phonetic reasons (the *ö >* *ü* change is natural in the Tkc. languages; the opposite direction is not).

We believe that the word comes from OTkc. **tög-* (~ **töv-*) 'to beat, to hit'. The differences in auslaut (low : high vowels) probably suggest two separate derivates from Tkc. *dög-* ~ *döv-* 'to beat, to hit'[44]:

---

44 Perhaps also Tat. *dügi* 'wheat' (cf.) speaks in favour of such a distinction.

1. in -*i*: **tögi* (> *döğü, tüvi, tügi* > *dügi* > *dügü* > *düğü* > *düjü* and *dugu*[45])
   Cf. e.g. *bini* 'broken (animal)', *biti* 'writing', *japy* 'building' (Zajączkowski 1932: 105)
2. in -*e*: **töge* (> *dögö, dŏğŏ*)
   Cf. e.g. *jara* 'wound', *jaja* 'rainbow', *tuda* 'handle', *üörä* 'happiness' (Pomorska 2004: 120, Zajączkowski 1932: 105).

For semantic development, cf. Slav. *proso* < **per-* 'to hit' ~ **pro-* + -*s*, i.e. 'something hit, something beaten' > 'husked millet grain' > 'millet grain' > 'grain' (Sędzik 1977: 11), and it is quite possible that this parallel is not coincidental. Anyway, it is interesting that millet (cf. *tögü* 'millet') came to Europe from the East (Nowiński 1970: 189). One might venture then, to suppose that the Slav. name is not entirely a native neologism, but rather a calque deriving eventually from some very old name, on which the Tkc. **tögi/e* is also based. Naturally, such a convergence also might be a purely coincidental one. The semantic development presented here is in fact, quite trivial.

Dövme 'wheat' provides a nice semantic parallel, too.

On the other hand, we should not discount the possibility that the name came from **tügī* 'hair (adj.)' < *tük* 'hair' + -*ī* adj. (< Pers.). While seemingly acceptable from the phonetic point of view (although the -*e*, -*ö* auslaut is unclear), this proposition raises some doubts on the semantic side. The meanings of 'hair' and 'millet' are quite close to each other (cf. *tüjtary* 'millet') but we know of no parallels for 'hair' and 'rice'. Such a shift does not seem to be impossible, though, as rice and some species of millet (especially setarias) look quite similar.

Both ideas seem probable but only the first one assumes a more likely **ö* in the first syllable, requires no further semantic assumptions (for which perhaps no parallels exist), and explains the meanings of 'husked rice' and 'husked millet' in a more natural way.

Cf. *tögü* 'millet' and *djugi* 'wheat', and (semantics) *dövme, ügür* and *tüjtary* 'millet'.

---

45 The reason for the harmony shift in Kmk. is unclear. Most probably it can be treated as a result of the front : back alternation which, while it definitely exists, has not yet been properly examined, and is therefore unpredictable.

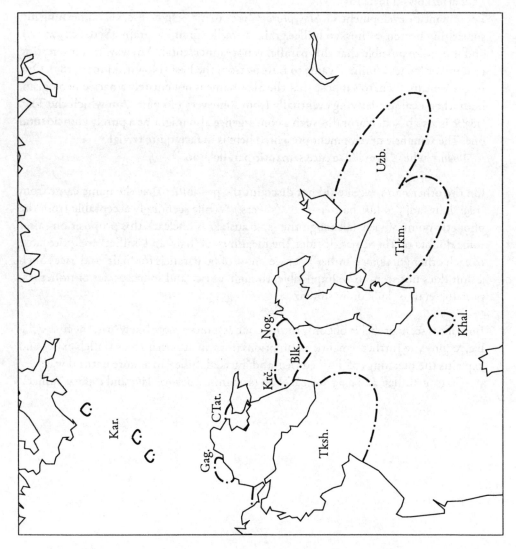

pirinč 'rice'

Rye is a secondary cultivable plant (formed from a weed), and is still found as a weed in some parts of the world, especially in the Indochinese and Central Asian Centres. Its requirements are rather moderate, allowing it to dominate in mountainous areas and in low quality soils, but it tends to be displaced by other plants in more fertile lands.

Rye probably originates from the area of Asia Minor, Iran and Armenia. Numerous primitive taxons with clearly weed-like features can still be found in the region and its surroundings. They surely can not have been ever been domesticated before as there never existed intentional cultivations of pure rye in this part of the world.

Seeds of rye turn out to be stronger when mixed with the seeds of other cereals. In Central Europe mixing equal amounts of rye and wheat, and then continuously seeding with the material of the same origin, results in nearly pure rye harvests in just a couple of years. It is probably this feature, in connection with a very old tradition of seeding mixtures of seeds rather than pure species, that gave birth to legends (Tkc., among others) of gradual change (a deterioration) of wheat into rye. (Nowiński 1970: 176–79.)

The relatively few names and their character (borrowings and descriptive names) show that rye has never been a particularly important plant for the Tkc. peoples. Presumably, it was treated, as it still often is in Asia, more as a weed than a cultivable plant.

FORMS:

ārəš → aryš	čovdor → čavdar	kök tarā → köktarā
ărša → aryš	dargan → darikan	kök tara → köktarā
arsānaj	darikan	köktarā
arys → aryš	darkān → darikan	oruos
aryš	jadagan → jadygan	qara buγdaj → kara bugdaj
aryš bidaj → aryš	jadygan	rožъ
aržanaj → arsānaj	jadygan aryš → jadygan	rži
aržanaj tarā → arsānaj	jatkan → jadygan	süle → suly
aržanaj taryg → arsānaj	jatkan aryš → aryš ‖ jadygan	sulli → suly
asłyk	kara bašak	suly
asłych → asłyk	kara bidaj → kara bugdaj	tereke → darikan
čadagan → jadygan	kara bijdaj → kara bugdaj	yraš → aryš
čadygan → jadygan	kara budaj → kara bugdaj	žavdar → čavdar
čavdar	kara būdaj → kara bugdaj	žavdar buγdoj → čavdar
čavdary → čavdar	kara-bugda → kara bugdaj	žavdari buγdoj → čavdar
čovdar → čavdar	kara bugdaj	žovdari → čavdar
čovdary → čavdar	kök najza	žaudar → čavdar

LANGUAGES:

Az.: *čovdar* || *čovdor*
Blk.: *kara budaj*
Brb.: *aryš*
Bšk.: *aryš*
Com.: *kara bugdaj*
Crm.: *čavdar*
CTat.: *aryš* || *čavdar*
Čuv.: *ărša* || *yraš*
Kar.: *aryš*
KarC: *aryš* || *čavdar*
KarH: *asłyk*
KarT: *ašłych*
Khak.: *arys* || *rožь*
Kirg.: *kara bijdaj* || *kara būdaj*
Kklp.: *arys* || *kara bidaj* || *kara bijdaj* || *sulli* || *suly*
Kmk.: *aryš* || *aryš bidaj* || *kara budaj*

Koyb.: *arys*
Krč.: *kara budaj*
Krč.Blk.: *arys* || *kara bijdaj* || *kara budaj*
Küär.: *aryš* || *jadygan aryš* || *jatkan* || *jatkan aryš*
Kyzyl: *ārəš*
Kzk.: *arys* || *aryš* || *kara bidaj* || *kök najza*
Leb.: *aryš*
Nog.: *arys* || *kara bijdaj* || *suly*
Ott.: *čavdar*
Oyr.: *aryš* || *jadagan*
Sag.: *arys* || *čadagan* || *jadygan*
Šr.: *aryš* || *čadygan* || *jadygan*
Tat.: *aryš* || *kara-bugda*
Tat.Gr.: *čavdar*

Tel.: *aryš*
Tksh.: *čavdar*
Tksh.dial.: *dargan* || *darikan* || *darkān* || *tereke*
Tob.: *aryš*
Tof.: *aržanaj* || *aržanaj tarā* || *aržanaj taryg*
Trkm.: *arys* || *aryš* || *čavdary* || *čovdar* || *čovdary* || *rožь* || *süle*
Tuv.: *kök tara* || *kök tarā* || *köktarā*
Uyg.: *kara bugdaj* || *qara buγdaj*
Uzb.: *žavdar* || *žavdar buγdoj* || *žavdari buγdoj* || *žaudar*
Yak.: *arsānaj* || *oruos*

ARSĀNAJ

FORMS:

arsānaj **Yak.**: Dmitrieva 1972
aržanaj **Tof.**: Anikin 2003 s.v. *ржаной*
aržanaj tarā **Tof.**: RTofS
aržanaj taryg **Tof.**: RTofS

LANGUAGES:

Tof.: *aržanaj, aržanaj tarā, aržanaj taryg* || **Yak.**: *arsānaj*

ETYMOLOGY:

1972: Dmitrieva: Yak. *arsānaj* < Russ.dial. Sib. *aržanoj* = Russ. *ržanoj* 'rye [adj.]'
2003: Anikin s.v. *ржаной*: Yak. *arsānaj* < Russ.dial. Sib. *a/oržanój* 'rye [adj.]'

COMMENTARY:

While we do not intend to negate the previous propositions, we believe they require a little more commentary.

Long vowel in the last but one syllable of the Yak. form is discordant with the Russ. accent. Such an adaptation can probably be explained by the fact that the Russ. adjective suffixes *-oj* and *-ój* are always treated in Yak. as non-accented, which allows for shifting the trace of the accent (the length of the vowel) to another syllable.

The connection with *tarā ~ taryg* in Tof. is probably a calque from a Russ.dial. compound *aržanó žito* 'rye', where *žito* 'cereal in sheafs; cereal in seeds; rye; wheat' (Fedotov 1979), although it is also possible that a very popular model in Tof. of naming cereals by composition with *tarā* could have played some role here as well, cf. *tarā* 'millet'.

ARYŠ

FORMS:

ārəš **Kyzyl:** Joki 1953

ărša **Čuv.:** Adjagaši 2005: 175 'зной и марево во время поспеванийа ржи'

arys **Khak.:** RChakS, Dmitrieva 1972, Achmetьjanov 1989: 48 || **Kklp.:** Achmetьja-nov 1989: 48 || **Koyb.:** VEWT, Anikin 2003 || **Krč.Blk.:** RKrčBlkS || **Kzk.:** RKzkS-54, Dmitrieva 1972, Achmetьjanov 1989: 48, DFKzk || **Nog.:** RNogS, Dmitrieva 1972 || **Sag.:** VEWT, Eren 1999 s.v. *çavdar*, Anikin 2003 || **Trkm.:** Dmitrieva 1972

aryš **Brb.:** R I 278b, Anikin 2003 || **Bšk.:** RBškS, Dmitrieva 1972, Achmetьjanov 1989: 48, Anikin 1998, Adjagaši 2005: 175 || **CTat.:** Achmetьjanov 1989: 48 || **Kar.:** אריש R I 278b, Achmetьjanov 1989: 48 || **KarC:** KRPS, Levi 1996 || **Kmk.:** Dmitrieva 1972 || **Küär.:** R I 278b, Anikin 2003 || **Kzk.:** VEWT 26a, DFKzk || **Leb.:** Anikin 2003 || **Oyr.:** R I 278b, RAltS, VEWT, Dmitrieva 1972, Achmetьjanov 1989: 48, Anikin 2003 || **Šr.:** R I 278b, Anikin 2003 || **Tat.:** Ima-naevъ 1901, VEWT, RTatS-G, Dmitrieva 1972, Achmetьjanov 1989: 48, Anikin 1998, Anikin 2003, Adjagaši 2005: 175 || **Tel.:** Ryumina-Sırkaşeva 1995, Eren 1999 s.v. *çavdar*, Anikin 2003 || **Tob.:** R I 278b, Anikin 2003 || **Trkm.:** Alijiv/Böörijif 1929

aryš bidaj **Kmk.:** RKmkS

jatkan aryš **Küär.:** R I 278b

yraš **Čuv.:** Nikolьskij 1909, RČuvS-D, RČuvS-E, RČuvS-A, VEWT, Dmitrieva 1972, Achmetьjanov 1989: 48, Adjagaši 2005: 175

LANGUAGES:

Brb.: *aryš* || **Bšk.:** *aryš* || **CTat.:** *aryš* || **Čuv.:** *ărša, yraš* || **Kar.:** *aryš* || **KarC.:** *aryš* || **Khak.:** *arys* || **Kklp.:** *arys* || **Kmk.:** *aryš, aryš bidaj* || **Koyb.:** *arys* || **Krč.Blk.:** *arys* || **Küär.:** *aryš, jatkan aryš* || **Kyzyl:** *ārəš* || **Kzk.:** *arys, aryš* || **Leb.:** *aryš* || **Nog.:** *arys* || **Oyr.:** *aryš* || **Sag.:** *arys* || **Šr.:** *aryš* || **Tat.:** *aryš* || **Tel.:** *aryš* || **Tob.:** *aryš* || **Trkm.:** *arys, aryš*

ETYMOLOGY:

1969: VEWT: *aryš* &c. < Russ. *rožь* 'rye'

1972: Dmitrieva: *aryš* &c., Čuv. *yraš*

1989: Achmetьjanov: 48: < ORuss. *rože*
Khak., Kzk. *arys* < [unclear expression] Bšk., CTat., Kar., Oyr., Tat. *aryš*
CTat., Kar. *aryš*, Khak., Kklp., Kzk. *arys* < Tat.

1996: Fedotov: *aryš* &c. (but *rožь* not listed) < Russ. *rožь* 'rye'

1998: Anikin RTur: Tat., Bšk. *aryš* < Russ. *rožь* 'rye'

1999: Eren s.v. *çavdar*: quotes VEWT

2003: Anikin: Bšk., Tat. *aryš* < Russ.

2005: Adjagaši: Čuv. *yraš* < OČuv. **áraš* < [late OERuss.? early ORuss.?] [rož'] < OESlav. *rъžь*
Bšk., Tat. *aryš* < MBšk., MTat. **aryš* < VBulgh.2 **aryš* < OESlav. *rъžь*

COMMENTARY:

We can see no reason to doubt the essential part of the etymology first proposed by VEWT, and later accepted by many scholars[46], but we believe that it needs to be slightly modified. Epentetic vowels are high in the Tkc. languages (cf. also *žehimien* 'barley'), and so, as has been pointed out by Achmetьjanov 1989: 48, Russ. *rožь* should rather yield an **yryš*[47]-like form. This is why we believe that it was not the liter. form that was the source of the borrowing, but a dial. form **arýž*[48] (ORuss. 12ᵗʰ c. *rъžь*), which we believe raises no doubts about the phonetics. The uniformity of the Tkc. forms might suggest that the word was borrowed very early, and preserved in an almost or completely unchanged form in various languages. However, such an early borrowing from Russ. is not very likely for cultural reasons. Given that it appears over a wide area, we would rather believe that it was borrowed repeatedly, and independently. This does not contradict with the proposed Russ.dial. etymon, as it is found in very many of Russ.dial.

As to the sounding of our word, the vocalism of the Yak. form is the only exception, resulting surely from it being borrowed independently.

The source of *rožь* is, obviously, Russ. *rožь*, too. This form only appears in Trkm. and Khak. In Trkm. it is probably a very young borrowing, and for the Khak. form, we can see two possible explanations:

1. the word was not borrowed for the second time; only its spelling was changed to the Russ. one although the pronunciation (especially among the less educated) most probably remained unchanged. This explanation seems to be more probable.
2. the word was borrowed for the second time. Such an explanation is possible due to the spelling which suggests a different sounding, but seems to be less probable due to the practice often used in the Soviet Union, of restoring the original spelling of Russ. borrowings in various languages.
   Cf. *rožь*.

ASŁYK

FORMS:
  asłyk **KarH:** Mardkowicz 1935, KRPS
  ašłych **KarT:** KRPS

---

46 Achmetьjanov 1989: 48 does not fully accept it but his argument is expressed unclearly. He mentions, however, an important phonetic detail, that OESlav. *rъžь* should not receive the protetic *a-* in the Tkc. languages; cf. below.

47 Or, less probably, as Achmetьjanov 1989: 48 suggests it, **yreš*.

48 Filin 1965– does not list such a form. He does list, however, *aržanój* 'rye [adj.]' in numerous dial., including Siberian ones. According to Barchudarov 1997, *aržanoj* is attested since the 13ᵗʰ c.
   The existence of Russ.dial. **aryž* is also suggested by Čuv. Anatri *ărša* 'зной и марево во время поспеванийа ржи' (Adjagaši 2005: 175) which could easily be explained by a borrowing of **arža* (**arša*?) in Gen.Sg., and by hardly anything else.

LANGUAGES:

 KarH.: *asłyk* || KarT.: *ašłych*

ETYMOLOGY: see *aš* 'barley'

COMMENTARY:

 We do not know of any semantic parallel for combining the meanings of 'rye' and 'barley' in one word. However, it is not necessarily surprising in this case, as the etymology of this word would allow it to develop quite freely.

ČAVDAR

FORMS:

 čavdar Crm.: جـاودار R III 1936m || CTat.: Zaatovъ 1906 || KarC: KRPS, Levi 1996 ||
  Ott.: جاودار R III 1936m, (چاودار) Wiesentahl 1895 || Tat.Gr.: Podolsky 1981 || Tksh.:
  Dmitrieva 1972

 čavdary Trkm.: Alijiv/Böörijif 1929

 čovdar Az.: RAzS, Dmitrieva 1972 || Trkm.: KTLS

 čovdary Trkm.: RTrkmS, Nikitin/Kerbabaev 1962, Dmitrieva 1972

 čovdor Az.: KTLS

 žavdar Uzb.: RUzbS-A, RUzbS-Š

 žavdar buɣdoj Uzb.: RUzbS-Š

 žavdari buɣdoj Uzb.: RUzbS-A

 žovdari Uzb.: Dmitrieva 1972

 žaudar Uzb.: Lapin 1899, Smolenskij 1912

LANGUAGES:

 Az.: *čovdar, čovdor* || Crm.: *čavdar* || CTat.: *čavdar* || KarC.: *čavdar* || Ott.: *čavdar* ||
 Tat.Gr.: *čavdar* || Tksh.: *čavdar* || Trkm.: *čavdary, čovdar, čovdary* || Uzb.: *žavdar, žavdar*
 buɣdoj, žavdari buɣdoj, žaudar

ETYMOLOGY:

 1969: VEWT: < Pers. *čūdār*

 1998: Stachowski, S.: < NPers. *čāvdār* 'rye (*Secale cereale*)'

 1999: Eren 1999: < Pers. *čūdār* 'rye', quoting for comparison Pers. *žaudar* 'a herb growing in wheat', *žaudara* 'a herb growing amongst wheat', *gaudar, gaudara* 'a plant
   growing amongst wheat and barley', *žau, žav* 'barley, a grain of barley'

COMMENTARY:

 1. VEWT's proposition, and its acceptance by Eren 1999 seems absolutely incomprehensible. In the modern liter. Pers., there exist two forms of this word: چـودار
  [-oу̯-] and چاودار [-āv-]. Even though the alternation of *oу̯ ~ av ~ ū* is quite common
  in Pers., we can see no reason to assume, as VEWT and Eren 1999 suggest it,
  a borrowing of the -*ū*- form when the Tkc. forms point clearly to the -*av*- one.

 2. The Tkc. alternation of -*a*- ~ -*o*- is probably to be explained by borrowings from
  different dialects of Pers. or, even more probably, from Taj. (Pers. *ā* = Taj. *o*;
  Pers. *a* = Taj. *a*).

- The Uyg. *ž-* in place of the expected *ǯ-* or *č-* is not clear to us, not least because in Uyg. (at least in its liter. version), all the three consonants exist in anlaut (see e.g. Tömür 2003).
- The Uzb. alternation of -*a*- / -*o*- ~ -*ä*- is presumably to be explained by the palatalizing influence of *č*, quite common in the Tkc. languages, and a secondary adaptation of the second syllable to the vowel harmony.
- In Trkm. and Uyg. there appears a final -*i* / -*y*. Although we cannot prove it directly, we suppose that they are of entirely different origin:
  - The Uyg. -*i* is an adjective suffix (cf. e.g. Uyg. ﺍﻗﺘﺴﺎﺩﻱ 'economical' or ﺍﻧﻘﻼﺑﻲ 'revolutionary' (Tömür 2003: 121f.)). (Lack of the *i* umlaut results from the original length of the vowel of the final syllable in the Pers. source; cf. Jarring 1933: 91: 'Der Vokal in dieser [final] Silbe ist immer *a* oder *u*'.)
  - The Trkm. final -*ry* could in theory be a harmonized version of **čavdari*, abstracted from a **čavdari bugdaj* (?)-like compound. Since, however, such a compound is not attested, the proposition of Eren 1999, to explain the final -*y* by a contamination with Trkm. *dary* 'millet', seems to be more probable. Such a solution would cast some light on the order in which the Tkc. peoples learned about these cereals; similarly *köktarā* (cf.) suggests such an ordering for Tuv.
3. On naming 'rye' with the name for 'wheat', cf. *kara bugdaj*.

DARIKAN

FORMS: *dargan, darikan, darkān, tereke* **Tksh.dial.:** Dankoff 1995: 702
ETYMOLOGY:
    1995: Dankoff: 702: < Arm. տարեկան *tarekan* 'rye'
    1999: Eren: < Arm. (after Dankoff 1995: 702)
COMMENTARY:
Dankoff's 1995: 72 etymology is probably true (although cf. also (Arm. >) Kurd. *tarigan*, Dankoff 1995: 702). His Arm. etymology also seems to be very plausible: < տարի *tari* 'year', liter. 'annual' > 'harvest' > 'rye', which easily explains such Tksh.dial. meanings as *tereke* 'cereal', *tereklik* 'vegetable garden' or *tereke* 'wheat' (cf.) &c., if assuming a borrowing from before the semantic shift in Arm. (attested in Ott. since the 14ᵗʰ c.).

JADYGAN

FORMS:
    čadagan **Sag.:** 'Winterrogen' VEWT 177a
    čadygan **Šr.:** VEWT 177a
    jadagan **Oyr.:** RAltS, Dmitrieva 1972
    jadygan **Sag.:** Eren 1999 s.v. *çavdar* ‖ **Šr.:** Eren 1999 s.v. *çavdar*, R III 211b
    jadygan aryš **Küär.:** R III 203b
    jatkan **Küär.:** R III 203b
    jatkan aryš **Küär.:** R I 278b

LANGUAGES:
Küär.: *jadygan aryš, jatkan, jatkan aryš* || **Oyr.**: *jadagan* || **Sag.**: *čadagan, jadygan* ||
Šr.: *čadygan, jadygan*
ETYMOLOGY: 1969: VEWT: < *jat-* 'to lie'
COMMENTARY:
The etymology proposed in VEWT is semantically plausible but it has some weaknesses, too:
- for:
  - **semantics:** Rye, being a weed, has more fragile stems, and ripens faster than cereals, thanks to which its seeds scatter very early, even before the harvest. Thus, on a field where wheat and rye grow together, broken rye stems are visible quite clearly among wheat. (Nowiński 1970: 178)
- against:
  - **suffixation:** Generally, the suffix used here has a form *-gan*, not *-Vgan*, and is consistently attached to nominal, not verbal, bases in the names of animals and plants. (Poppe 1927: 116; Frankle 1948: 55f.).
  - **distribution:** If *-gan* was indeed the suffix used here, Küär. would be the only language to preserve its original form. This is not very likely since Küär. is not a peripheral language and it does not preserve such old forms very often.
  The possibility exists, however, of a partial defence against the objection from the point suffixation: the appearance of *-y-* (*-a-* in Sag. *čadagan* is surely secondary (< **čadygan*) and results from the not fully clear alternation of *a ~ y*) could have been caused by an analogy to quite numerous derivates in *-gan(a)* from roots ending in *-y*. They are also common in the Mo. languages which influenced quite heavily the Tkc. languages with the *-y-* forms: cf. Mo. *üni-jen* < *üni-gen* 'cow', *kulu-gana* 'mouse' (Poppe 1927: 116). Besides, *-a-* in Sag. *čadagan*, too, could be explained by an analogy to Mo. forms such as *kila-gana* 'a species of steppe grass', *üne-gen* 'fox', *teme-gen* 'camel' (Poppe 1927: 116). This is probably how the Brb. form *küzügän* 'eagle' came into existence: < *küc* 'eagle with a white tail' (Frankle 1948: 55f.).
  Still, this defence does not explain why such a derivate should be made from a verbal, and not a nominal, stem. In theory, one could assume that an unknown nominal **jat* was in fact the base, and it would not be an unacceptable assumption as this is actually the case with most names of animals and plants with the *-gan* suffix, cf. Poppe's opinion (1927: 116): 'Was dieses Suffix *-yan* ursprünglich bedeutete und welche Funktion es hatte, ist unbekannt, da entsprechende Stämme sonst in der Sprache nicht vorkommen'.
Perhaps the unknown **jat* could be identified with Čag., Kar., Oyr., Tat., Uyg. *jat* 'foreign, strange' R III 190b? Then the meaning would have to be something like 'foreign cereal'. Unfortunately, it seems to be impossible to determine when the Sag., Šr. and Küär. became acquainted with rye.[49]

---

49 Although it seems to be at least possible to say for Küär. that the words *jatkan ~ jadygan* must be older than *aryš*, i.e. older than perhaps the 17th c. (or maybe even older?). This is not, however,

However, 'foreign, strange' could also be understood as 'not sown, and still appearing' rather than 'coming from someone foreign'. Then, such a derivate would be understandable, given the weed-like character of rye. This explanation seems to be quite likely but very difficult to prove.

Finally, it might also be that it is not the above mentioned *jat* 'foreign, strange' that explains our word, but some unattested semantic change such as Čul. *Šat ~ č-* 'Tatar' (Stachowski, M. 1998: 116). But whether the Sag., Šr. and Küär. became acquainted with rye from the Tatars, is unknown. A semantic parallel could be provided by Pol. *tatarka* 'a species of groats', *gryka* and others (cf. also Mańczak 1999: 95f.).

Yet another possibility would be to assume the existence of some unknown nominal stem *jady*. The fact that such a stem is unknown would not in itself be a strong argument against such a proposition. However, the Küär. form of *jatkan* would then become quite incomprehensible. Perhaps the most probable explanation would be to assume that the word had been shortened in Küär., which is a fairly common phenomenon with three-syllable words with a high vowel in the middle syllable.

Additionally, it is rather puzzling that none of the above propositions can explain the concurrent existence of *j-* and *č-* forms in Sag. and Šr. Generally, *č-* is the counterpart of Tkc. *j-* in these languages, including in borrowings, e.g. Sag. *čablak* 'potato' < Russ. *jabloko* (Räsänen 1949: 162). Perhaps the most likely explanation is that of a late borrowing, and most probably from Oyr.

There exist in fact three explanations of our word, and none of them are wholly convincing:
1. *jat-* 'to lie'; **for:** semantics; **against:** suffixation (partial possibility of defence), distribution
2. *jat-* nominal (*jat* 'foreign, strange'); **for:** semantics; **against:** phonetics (-*ygan*)
3. *jady-* nominal; **for:** phonetics, suffixation; **against:** not attested (not a very strong argument), Küär. *jatkan*[50]

Most probably, this derivate is very old, as is suggested by the facts that the base is utterly unclear, and that the derivational model is nowadays essentially unproductive. The possibility of a very old borrowing, adapted both morphologically and phonetically, cannot be ultimately discounted. Determining the exact period of borrowing seems, however, to be impossible given the complete lack of old, and abundant, data.

---

a very important clue since the cultural data show that rye should have been known in this region much earlier.

50 Although one can not definitively exclude the possibility of a later, irregular change in Küär. caused probably by folk etymology and an association with *jat* 'foreign, strange'? 'to lie'?

KARA BAŠAK

FORMS: *kara bašak* **Ott.**: R IV 1551b
ETYMOLOGY: as yet not discussed
COMMENTARY:

Literary 'worse ear'; on *kara* cf. *kara bugdaj*. This is understandable, given that rye was for a very long time, and sometimes still is regarded, as being a weed rather than a cereal.

KARA BUGDAJ

FORMS:

kara bidaj **Kklp.**: RKklpS-BB, Dmitrieva 1972 || **Kzk.**: RKzkS-46, RKzkS-54, Dmitrieva 1972, DFKzk

kara bijdaj **Kirg.**: Mašanovъ 1899 || **Kklp.**: RKklpS-ST, RKklpS-B || **Krč.Blk.**: RKrčBlkS || **Nog.**: RNogS, Dmitrieva 1972

kara budaj **Blk.**: Németh 1911/12: 129 || **Kmk.**: Németh 1911/12: 129 || **Krč.**: Pröhle 1909: 95 || **Krč.Blk.**: Dmitrieva 1972

kara būdaj **Kirg.**: RKirgS-Ju44, RKirgS-Ju57, Dmitrieva 1972

kara-bugda **Tat.**: قارا بوغدا Tanievъ 1909

kara bugdaj **Com.**: R IV 1807b || **Uyg.**: KTLS

qara buɣdaj **Uyg.**: قارا بوغداي RUjgS

LANGUAGES:

Blk.: *kara budaj* || **Com.**: *kara bugdaj* || **Kirg.**: *kara bijdaj, kara būdaj* || **Kklp.**: *kara bidaj, kara bijdaj* || **Kmk.**: *kara budaj* || **Krč.**: *kara budaj* || **Krč.Blk.**: *kara bijdaj, kara budaj* || **Kzk.**: *kara bidaj* || **Nog.**: *kara bijdaj* || **Tat.**: *kara-bugda* || **Uyg.**: *kara bugdaj, qara buɣdaj*

ETYMOLOGY:

1961: Laude-Cirtautas 1961: describes the metaphorical meaning of *kara* as 'usual, common; of lower quality' when dealing with its usage in plant names (see 34f.), and exemplifies it with Blk., Kmk. *kara budaj*, Com., Uyg. *kara buɣdaj* meaning 'wheat of lower quality'

1972: Dmitrieva: < *kara* 'black' + *bugdaj*[51]

COMMENTARY:

This name is a composition of two words, both of which requires a separate explanation.

KARA:

We can see two possibilities of explaining the usage of *kara* here:

1. according to the description proposed by Laude-Cirtautas 1961: 34f. This option is very plausible, especially because using the names of colours metaphorically is quite common in the Tkc. languages, and also because rye has never been highly regarded in Asia, to the extent that it is often considered to be a weed.

2. by linking it with ergot (*Secale cornutum*), i.e. sclerotium of a parasitic fungus in the genus *Claviceps*, which attacks rye among others, and can be noticed as little black

---

51 In Dmitrieva 1972, only the etymology of Kirg. *kara būdaj* is given directly, but we believe it should be assumed that it concerns all the names of this kind which are quoted here.

spots on the ears. This possibility appears to be less probable as 1. ergot attacks wheat, too (though less commonly); 2. it seems quite strange, that the name of a cereal should be derived from a fungus which attacks it, and is therefore a symptom of an illness and not an integral part of the plant.

BUGDAJ:

Calling rye with a name for 'wheat' can be explained in two planes:

1. **biological:** Rye behaves as a weed, i.e. it grows on the fields where other cereals had been sown, very often on fields of wheat. Because it ripens faster, and its stems are more fragile and break earlier, it soon equals the sown cereals in number, or even surpass them.

2. **ethnographical:** In connection with the above, the Tkc. peoples, who never greatly appreciated rye, have developed legends about wheat gradually turning (deteriorating) into rye. This fact shows clearly the relative order in which the Tkc. peoples became acquainted with these cereals, and is also supported by the fact that while the name *bugdaj* 'wheat' is widespread, and is native or borrowed as early as the PTkc. period (or even earlier, perhaps?), the names for 'rye' are more numerous and are all descriptive (including by comparison to wheat) or borrowed in the historic times.

KÖK NAJZA

FORMS: *kök najza* **Kzk.**: R III 635m
ETYMOLOGY: as yet not discussed
COMMENTARY:

The meaning of *kök* is not entirely clear here. For certain, it is more about a shade of green rather than blue: rye does not have a blue tint, neither as a plant nor as a grain. It is also possible, though, that this word is not used as a simple colour name here. Given that rye is often considered to be an inferior type of cereal, perhaps we should assume a semantic development such as 'green' > 'unripe' > 'inferior', even if, to the best of our knowledge, there is no attestation of such a shift. At least in respect to animals, *kök* can have meanings far from 'blue' or 'green', e.g. 'gray', 'silver' and even Uzb. *kök koj* 'brown sheep' (Laude-Cirtautas 1961: 79).

Kzk. *najza* means 'lance' and is derived (VEWT) from Pers. نايـزه *nāyze* (~ نايزه *nāyže*) '1. bronchus; 2. bugle, tube'. The usage of this word is not accidental; the hair on the ears of rye is exceptionally stiff and prickly.

KÖKTARĀ

FORMS:

   kök tarā **Tuv.**: Dmitrieva 1972 || *kök tara* Dmitrieva 1979
   köktarā **Tuv.**: RTuwS

ETYMOLOGY:

   1972: Dmitrieva: < *kök* 'blue' + *tarā* 'grain'
   1979: Dmitrieva: liter. 'dark millet'
      Assuming the meaning of 'blue' rather than 'green' seems to be strange. To the best of our knowledge, no cereal or its grains are blue. Cf. *kök najza.*

COMMENTARY:
Literary 'green grain (?)'. On *kök* see *kök najza*.

Tarā corresponds to Tkc. *dary* 'millet' (see) and means in Tuv. '1. cereal; 2. grain; 3. millet'. It is difficult to determine with any certainty which is the meaning employed in this case.

'Grain' seems to be the most probable one. Grains of rye do indeed have a green tint to them, more clearly visible than with other cereals. This is not, however, enough, to exclude all the other possibilities. If we assumed a semantic development such as with *kök najza*, the meaning of 'inferior cereal' would seem to render the attitude of the Tkc. peoples towards rye quite accurately.

Finally, one can not rule out the possibility that the meaning used here is 'millet', and that the whole name is but another confirmation of the fact the Tkc. peoples became acquainted with rye after wheat. The last possibility seems, however, to be the least probable.

ORUOS

FORMS: *oruos* **Yak.**: Slepcov 1964: 37, 92, RJakS, Dmitrieva 1972, Anikin 2003
ETYMOLOGY: 1972: Dmitrieva: < Russ. *rožь* 'rye'
COMMENTARY:
Dmitrieva 1972's etymology appears to be true, and requires no further commentary.

ROŽЬ

FORMS:
rožь **Khak.**: RChakS, Dmitrieva 1972 || **Trkm.**: RTrkmS, (scientific) Nikitin/Kerbabaev 1962
LANGUAGES:
Khak.: *rožь* || **Trkm.**: *rožь*
ETYMOLOGY: as yet not discussed
COMMENTARY: < Russ. *rožь* 'rye'. Cf. *aryš*.

RŽI

FORMS: *rži* **Bšk.**: Dmitrieva 1972
ETYMOLOGY: as yet not discussed
COMMENTARY: < Russ. *rži* Gen. < *rožь* 'rye'. Cf. also *prosa* 'millet'.

SULY

FORMS:
süle **Trkm.**: (Kopet-Dag) Nikitin/Kerbabaev 1962
sulli **Kklp.**: RKklpS-BB
suly **Kklp.**: RKklpS-B || **Nog.**: Eren 1999 s.v. *çavdar*

LANGUAGES:
  Kklp.: *sulli, suly* ‖ **Nog.**: *suly* ‖ **Trkm.**: *süle*
ETYMOLOGY: see *saly* 'rice'
COMMENTARY:
  This word is widespread in the Tkc. languages, but usually in the meaning of 'rice'.
Also in Kklp. it is present in this meaning, in the form of *saly*.
  The unusual meaning here might result simply from a lack of orientation or, less
probably, from the weed-like character of rye; cf. *budaj* (although rye grows mostly in
fields of wheat, not rice).

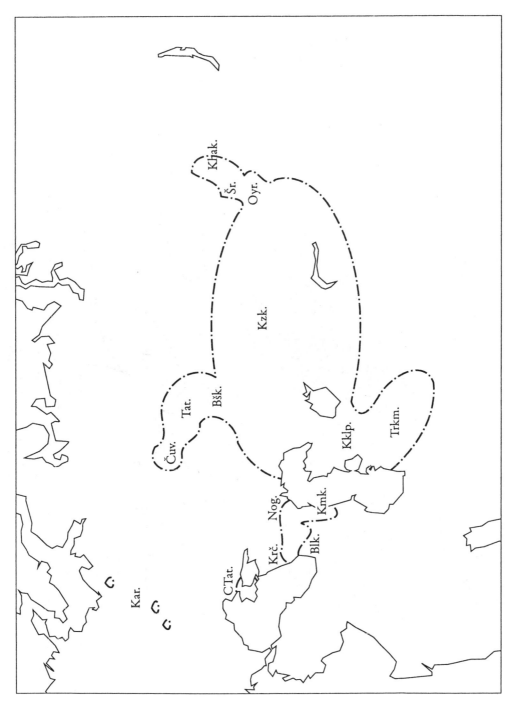

aryš 'rye'

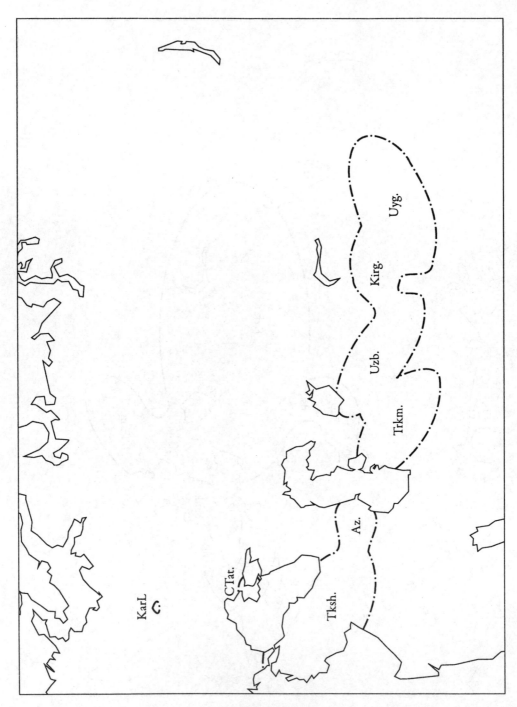

čavdar 'rye'

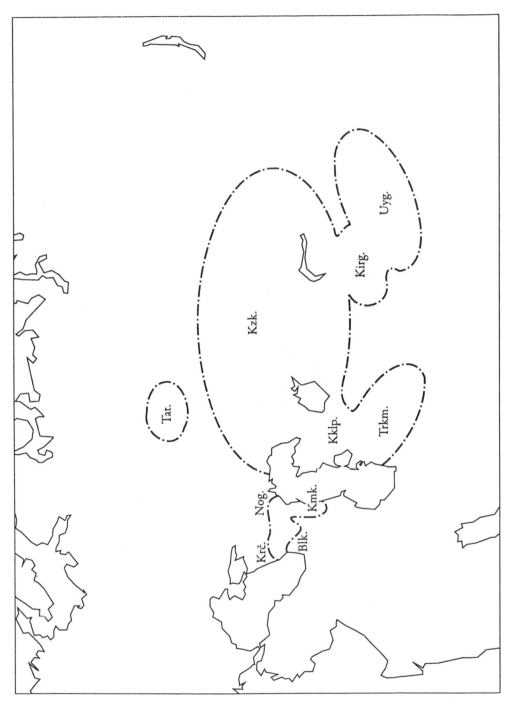

kara bugdaj 'rye'

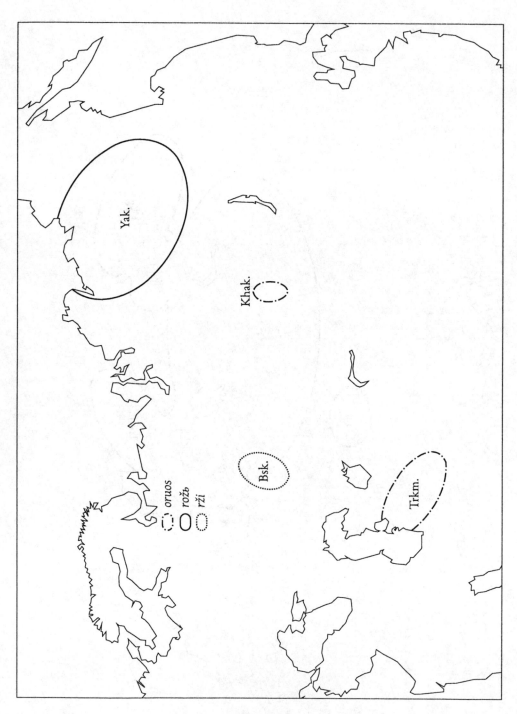

rožь 'rye'

Wheat is one of the oldest, perhaps the oldest, and also perhaps the most important cereal of the world. The Triticum genus is composed of numerous species and varieties. Despite the unusually long history of cultivation, wheat can still often be found growing wildly.

It is very difficult to determine exactly when the cultivation of wheat began. The oldest grains of *Triticum dioccum* are dated seven thousand years BC. The domestication probably happened in Egypt and/or in the Fertile Crescent. It spread to Europe, North Africa and Asia as early as the time of the primitive farming cultures, even thousands of years BC (Nowiński 1970: 155). The oldest of the cultivated species of wheat is *Triticum dioccum*, once very widespread in Asia and elsewhere, and originating probably from the region of Syria and Palestine. Another once very popular species is spelt (*T. spelta*). Its origin is not fully understood but it is probable that it came into being in Central-Eastern or Eastern Asia. Nowadays, common wheat (or bread wheat; *T. vulgare* = *T. aestivum*) is definitely the most popular. It originates from the Middle East and is over four and a half thousand years old. It displaced all the other species to a considerable degree.

Among the Tkc. names for 'wheat', *buɡdaj* is very clearly the most common. This fact can be interpreted as an indication that the Tkc. and Mo. peoples became acquainted with wheat very long ago, perhaps before the decay of the Tkc.Mo. union[52]. The absence of the word from the Ma.Tung. languages (not counting a later borrowing from Mo.) only confirms the relative chronology of the decay of the Alt. union.

FORMS:

aktarā	bogdaj → bugdaj	buddaj → bugdaj
astyɣ → aš(lyk)	bögdaj → bugdaj	budgaj → bugdaj
aš → aš(lyk)	bögdoj → bugdaj	būdoj → bugdaj
ašlik → aš(lyk)	bōɡōdaj → bugdaj	bugda → bugdaj
ašlyk → aš(lyk)	boɣdaj → bugdaj	bugdaj
bidaj → bugdaj	bojdaj → bugdaj	bugdāj → bugdaj
bīdaj → bugdaj	bojδaj → bugdaj	buɣdaj → bugdaj
bijdaj → bugdaj	bojzaj → bugdaj	buɣdoj → bugdaj
bodaj → bugdaj	boraj → bugdaj	buɣudaj → bugdaj
bödåj → buɡdaj	böraj → bugdaj	bujdaj → bugdaj
bōdaj → bugdaj	böråj → bugdaj	bujδaj → bugdaj
bödoj → bugdaj	budaj → bugdaj	buldej → bugdaj
böδaj → bugdaj	bŭdaj → bugdaj	buraj → bugdaj
bogda → bugdaj	būdaj → bugdaj	būtaj → bugdaj

---

52 We use the term *union* here to avoid the discussion on what was its exact character.

buvdaj → bugdaj
dövme
dügi
genim
göže
hinta
jasmyk
kyzyl bodaj
kyzyl tas → kyzyltas
kyzyltas

mejzə
öjür
pări → bugdaj
pogtə → bugdaj
pöri → bugdaj
pŏri → bugdaj
pūdaj → bugdaj
pugdaj → bugdaj
seliehinej
seliesenej → seliehinej

seliesinej → seliehinej
šenīse
šīse → šenīse
šĩse → šenīse
taryg
tereke
tula
tulă → tula

LANGUAGES:

Az.: *bugda*
Blk.: *budaj*
Brb.: *pugdaj*
Bšk.: *bodaj* ‖ *bödåj* ‖ *böδaj* ‖
    bojδaj ‖ *bojzaj* ‖ *boraj* ‖
    bujδaj ‖ *buraj*
Com.: *bugdaj*
CTat.: *bogdaj* ‖ *budgaj*
Čag.: *bogdaj* ‖ *budgaj* ‖
    bugdaj
Čuv.: *pări* ‖ *pöri* ‖ *pŏri* ‖
    tula ‖ *tulă*
Fuyü: *mejzə*
Gag.: *bodaj* ‖ *bōdaj* ‖ *bŭdaj*
    ‖ *tereke*
Kar.: *bogdaj* ‖ *budgaj*
KarC: *bogdaj*
KarH: *budaj*
KarT: *budaj*
Khak.: *pugdaj*
Khal.: *bogda* ‖ *bugda*
Kirg.: *bijdaj* ‖ *būdaj* ‖ *bujdaj*
    ‖ *pūdaj*
Kklp.: *bidaj* ‖ *bijdaj* ‖ *būdaj*
    ‖ *buvdaj*

Kmk.: *bidaj* ‖ *budaj*
Krč.Blk.: *bidaj* ‖ *budaj*
Küär.: *pūdaj*
Kzk.: *bidaj* ‖ *bīdaj* ‖ *bijdaj* ‖
    boraj ‖ *bugdaj* ‖ *bujdaj*
MTkc.H: *bodaj* ‖ *bogdaj* ‖
    budaj ‖ *bugdaj*
MTkc.IM: *bugdaj*
MTkc.KM: *bugda* ‖ *bugdaj*
MTkc.MA.B: *bugdaj*
MTkc.MK: *ašlyk* ‖ *bugdāj*
    ‖ *taryg*
Nog.: *bijdaj*
Oghuz.Ir.: *bugda*
OTkc.: *budgaj* ‖ *bugdaj* ‖ *öjür*
Ott.: *bogdaj* ‖ *bojdaj* ‖
    budgaj ‖ *hinta*
OUyg.: *ašlyk*
Oyr.: *aš* ‖ *būdaj* ‖ *būdoj* ‖
    pūdaj
Oyr.dial.: *būtaj*
Sal.: *bogdaj* ‖ *bŭdaj* ‖ *pogtə*
Šr.: *bugdaj* ‖ *pūdaj*
Tat.: *bodaj* ‖ *bödåj* ‖ *bōdaj* ‖
    bödoj ‖ *bögdaj* ‖ *bögdoj* ‖

bōgōdaj ‖ *boraj* ‖ *böraj* ‖
    böråj ‖ *bŭdaj* ‖ *bugda* ‖
    dügi ‖ *kyzyl bodaj*
Tat.Gr.: *bogdaj*
Tel.: *pūdaj*
Tksh.: *bugda* ‖ *bugdaj* ‖
    dövme ‖ *göže*
Tksh.dial.: *buldej* ‖ *genim*
Tob.: *bugdaj* ‖ *bujdaj*
Tof.: *šenīse* ‖ *šīse* ‖ *šĩse*
Trkm.: *bogdaj* ‖ *budgaj*
Tuv.: *aktarā* ‖ *budaj* ‖ *bŭdaj*
    ‖ *būtaj* ‖ *kyzyl tas* ‖
    kyzyltas ‖ *pūdaj*
Uyg.: *ašlyk* ‖ *boγdaj* ‖
    buγdaj ‖ *buγdoj* ‖
    buγudaj
Uzb.: *astyγ* ‖ *ašlik* ‖ *buddaj*
    ‖ *bugdaj* ‖ *buγdoj*
Uzb.dial.: *buvdaj* ‖ *jasmyk*
Yak.: *seliehinej* ‖ *seliesenej* ‖
    seliesinej

AKTARĀ

FORMS: *aktarā* **Tuv.:** RTuwS, Dmitrieva 1972
ETYMOLOGY: 1972: Dmitrieva: < *ak* 'white' + *tarā* 'grain; cereal'

COMMENTARY:

This name is absolutely clear morphologically; it needs, however, a brief semantic explanation missing from Dmitrieva 1972.

Tarā corresponds to Tkc. *dary* 'millet' (cf.), here probably in the meaning of 'cereal' rather than 'millet'. *Ak* is presumably to be understood metaphorically, as 'good, better' which would be connected to the high importance attached to wheat.

Calling wheat with the name for 'millet' should indicate the order in which the Tuvinians became acquainted with these cereals. However, the data from the remaining Tkc. languages shows that wheat was probably the first cereal known to the Tkc. peoples. Perhaps millet took over the role of being the most important cereal for the Tuvinians, and this is where a secondary name for 'wheat' comes from? Cf. also *köktarā*.

AŠ(LYK)

FORMS:

astyy **Uzb.**: Çevilek 2005
aš **Oyr.**: Çevilek 2005
ašlik **Uzb.**: Çevilek 2005
ašlyk **MTkc.MK**: Dankoff/Kelly 1982–85 || **OUyg.**: Çevilek 2005 || **Uyg.**: Çevilek 2005

LANGUAGES:

MTkc.MK: *ašlyk* || **OUyg.:** *ašlyk* || **Oyr.:** *aš* || **Uyg.:** *ašlyk* || **Uzb.:** *astyy, ašlik*

ETYMOLOGY: see *as* 'barley'

COMMENTARY:

Given the original meaning of *aš*, 'soup', the fact that this word means both 'wheat' and 'barley' is no surprise, even in the absence of semantic parallels. The suffix *-lyk* is probably not used here in its most common meaning of 'abstractum', cf. the following characteristic: 'The suffix *-łyx, -lik, -łux, -luk* is in Karaim productive and forms denominal verbs denoting abstract concepts (nomina abstracta), also names of people (originally names of status, posts), things, and especially of plants, cf. e.g. *almałyx* 'apple-tree', *borłałyx* 'grapevine' and others.' (Zajączkowski 1932: 30f.; own translation). We believe that this information is relevant to other Tkc. languages, too.[53]

BUGDAJ

FORMS:

bidaj **Kklp.**: RKklpS-BB, Dmitrieva 1972 || **Kmk.**: RKmkS || **Krč.Blk.**: RKrčBlkS || **Kzk.**: RKzkS-46, RKzkS-54, Dmitrieva 1972, DFKzk
bīdaj **Kzk.**: Joki 1952
bijdaj **Kirg.**: Mašanovъ 1899 || **Kklp.**: RKklpS-ST, RKklpS-B || **Kzk.**: VEWT || **Nog.**: RNogS, Dmitrieva 1972

---

53 Cf. Čul. *aŋnyk* '1. trap, 2. morel' (Pomorska 2004: 74) << *aŋ* 'wild animal, beast' (Birjukovič 1984: 13), although in this case the meaning of 'morel' evolved probably from the meaning of 'trap' rather than 'wild animal'.

bodaj **Bšk.**: Brands 1973: 45 || **Gag.**: Güngör/Argunşah 1991 || **MTkc.H** || **Tat.**: Voskresenskij 1894, RTatS-D, Brands 1973: 45, RTatS-G

bödåj **Bšk.**: Joki 1952 || **Tat.**: Joki 1952

bōdaj **Gag.**: ÈSTJa, Dmitrieva 1972, Güngör/Argunşah 1991 || **Tat.**: Imanaevъ 1901, VEWT

bödoj **Tat.**: ÈSTJa

böδaj **Bšk.**: VEWT

bogda **Khal.**: Doerfer/Tezcan 1980

bogdaj **CTat.**: Zaatovъ 1906, ÈSTJa || **Čag.**: Joki 1952 || **Kar.**: ÈSTJa || **KarC**: KRPS, Levi 1996 || **MTkc.H** || **Ott.**: Joki 1952, VEWT || **Sal.**: Dmitrieva 1972, ÈSTJa || **Tat.Gr.**: Podolsky 1981 || **Trkm.**: Joki 1952, VEWT

bögdaj **Tat.**: Joki 1952

bögdoj **Tat.**: ÈSTJa

bōgōdaj **Tat.**: Imanaevъ 1901

boydaj **Uyg.**: Raquette 1927, ÈSTJa

bojdaj **Ott.**: Joki 1952

bojδaj **Bšk.**: Dmitrieva 1972, RBškS, Brands 1973: 45

bojzaj **Bšk.**: Fedotov 1996 s.v. *pări*

boraj **Bšk.**: 'spelt' Fedotov 1996 s.v. *pări* || **Kzk.**: VEWT, Räsänen 1946: 198 (~ *bijdajy*) || **Tat.**: 'spelt' Fedotov 1996 s.v. *pări*

böraj **Tat.**: VEWT

böråj **Tat.**: Räsänen 1946: 198

budaj **Blk.**: ÈSTJa || **KarH**: KRPS, Mardkowicz 1935 || **KarT**: KRPS, Kowalski 1929 || **Kmk.**: Dmitrieva 1972 || **Krč.Blk.**: Joki 1952, Dmitrieva 1972, ÈSTJa || **MTkc.H** || **Tuv.**: Tatarincev 2000–

bŭdaj **Gag.**: ÈSTJa || **Sal.**: ÈSTJa || **Tat.**: ÈSTJa || **Tuv.**: Tatarincev 2000–

būdaj **Kirg.**: RKirgS-Ju44, Joki 1952, RKirgS-Ju57, Dmitrieva 1972, ÈSTJa || **Kklp.**: Joki 1952 || **Oyr.**: Dmitrieva 1972, ÈSTJa, RAltS

buddaj **Uzb.**: Witczak 2003: 95

budgaj **CTat.**: Joki 1952 || **Čag.**: Joki 1952 || **Kar.**: Joki 1952 || **OTkc.**: DTS (one attestation in MK) || **Ott.**: Joki 1952 || **Trkm.**: Joki 1952

būdoj **Oyr.**: ÈSTJa

bugda **Az.**: Dmitrieva 1972, RAzS || **Khal.**: Doerfer/Tezcan 1980, Doerfer 1987 || **MTkc.MK** || **Oghuz.Ir.**: Doerfer/Hesche 1989 || **Tat.**: بوغدا Tanievъ 1909 || **Tksh.**: Tietze 2002–

bugdaj **Com.**: Fedotov 1996 s.v. *pări* || **Čag.**: Joki 1952, Fedotov 1996 s.v. *pări* || **Kzk.**: Fedotov 1996 s.v. *pări* || **MTkc.H** || **MTkc.IM** || **MTkc.MA.B**: Borovkov 1971: 100 || **MTkc.KM** || **OTkc.**: DTS (four attestations in MK), Dmitrieva 1972 || **Šr.**: Joki 1952 || **Tob.**: Joki 1952 || **Tksh.**: Dmitrieva 1972 || **Uzb.**: Nalivkinъ 1895 (بغداى), Lapin 1899, Smolenskij 1912, Alijiv/Böörijif 1929, RTrkmS, Nikitin/Kerbabaev 1962, Dmitrieva 1972

bugdāj **MTkc.MK**: Dankoff /Kelly 1982–85

buγdaj **Uyg.**: بوغداي RUjgSR, Dmitrieva 1972, Fedotov 1996 s.v. *pări*

buɣdoj **Uyg.:** RUjgSA || **Uzb.:** RUzbS-A, RUzbS-Š, Dmitrieva 1972
buɣudaj **Uyg.:** Menges 1933, ÈSTJa
bujdaj **Kirg.:** Mašanovъ 1899 || **Kzk.:** Joki 1952, VEWT || **Tob.:** VEWT
bujδaj **Bšk.:** ÈSTJa
buldej **Tksh.dial.:** UA
buraj **Bšk.:** Räsänen 1946: 198, VEWT
būtaj **Oyr.dial.:** ÈSTJa || **Tuv.:** Tatarincev 2000–
buvdaj **Kklp.:** Tatarincev 2000– || **Uzb.dial.:** ÈSTJa
pări **Čuv.:** Anatri 'spelt', Róna-Tas 1990: 31
pogtə **Sal.:** ÈSTJa
pöri **Čuv.:** 'spelt' VEWT
pöri **Čuv.:** Virjal Róna-Tas 1990: 31
pūdaj **Kirg.:** Joki 1952 || **Küär.:** Joki 1952 || **Oyr.:** Joki 1952, ÈSTJa || **Šr.:** Joki 1952 ||
     Tel.: Ryumina-Sırkaşeva 1995 || **Tuv.:** Tatarincev 2000–
pugdaj **Brb.:** VEWT || **Khak.:** Dmitrieva 1972, RChakS

LANGUAGES:

Az.: *bugda* || Blk.: *budaj* || Brb.: *pugdaj* || Bšk.: *bodaj, bödåj, böδaj, bojδaj, bojzaj, boraj, bujδaj, buraj* || Com.: *bugdaj* || CTat.: *bogdaj, budgaj* || Čag.: *bogdaj, budgaj, bugdaj* || Čuv.: *pări, pöri, pöri* || Gag.: *bodaj, bōdaj, bŭdaj* || Kar.: *bogdaj, budgaj* || KarC.: *bogdaj* || KarH: *budaj* || KarT: *budaj* || Khak.: *pugdaj* || Khal.: *bogda, bugda* || Kirg.: *bijdaj, būdaj, bujdaj, pūdaj* || Kklp.: *bidaj, bijdaj, būdaj, buvdaj* || Kmk.: *bidaj, budaj* || Krč.Blk.: *bidaj, budaj* || Küär.: *pūdaj* || Kzk.: *bidaj, bīdaj, bijdaj, boraj, bugdaj, bujdaj* || MTkc.H: *bodaj, bogdaj, budaj, bugdaj* || MTkc.IM: *bugdaj* || MTkc.KM: *bugda, bugdaj* || MTkc.MA.B: *bugdaj* || MTkc.MK: *bugdāj* || Nog.: *bijdaj* || Oghuz.Ir.: *bugda* || OTkc.: *budgaj, bugdaj* || Ott.: *bogdaj, bojdaj, budgaj* || Oyr.: *būdaj, būdoj, pūdaj* || Oyr.dial.: *būtaj* || Sal.: *bogdaj, bŭdaj, pogtə* || Šr.: *bugdaj, pūdaj* || Tat.: *bodaj, bödåj, bōdaj, bödoj, bögdaj, bögdoj, bōgōdaj, boraj, böraj, böråj, bŭdaj, bugda* || Tat.Gr.: *bogdaj* || Tel.: *pūdaj* || Tksh.: *bugda, bugdaj* || Tksh.dial.: *buldej* || Tob.: *bugdaj, bujdaj* || Trkm.: *bogdaj, budgaj* || Tuv.: *budaj, bŭdaj, būtaj, pūdaj* || Uyg.: *boɣdaj, buɣdaj, buɣdoj, buɣudaj* || Uzb.: *buddaj, bugdaj, buɣdoj* || Uzb.dial.: *buvdaj*

ETYMOLOGY (an overview of the most important propositions):

Ткс. *bugdaj*:

   1946: Räsänen: 198: Bšk. *buråj*, Kzk. *boraj-bijdajy*, Tat. *böråj* < Čuv. *păry* &c.

   1952: Joki: < OChin. *m^wɒk* 'wheat' or OChin.N. *m^wok* id. + OChin. *lậi* 'wheat'[54]
         Tkc. *budɣaj* is a metathesis; Mo. ~ (or <?) Tkc.
         Both words are attested in Chin. in the oldest monuments of the Yin period. The old Chin.N form *m^wok* is derived by being based on Mand. *mo*. The change *-gl-* > *-gd-* as in Nog. *čiglāk*, Trkm. *čigelek* 'Erdbeere' ~ MTkc. *jigdä* 'rote Brustbeere'. This proposition should be treated as obsolete now. Currently, Mand. *mai^+* is derived from MChin. *mEk* < OChin. *mrik* 'wheat'; OChin. *lậi* is probably to be understood as modern *li^+*, as in *mai^+li^+* 'wheat grain', which however < OChin. *C-rip* (oral information from Prof. A. Vovin [Honolulu]).

---

54 The compound *m^wɒk lậi* is written without an asterisk. This is probably supposed to mean that both its components are attested, as opposed to *m^wok-lậi* where the first element is reconstructed (writing with or without hyphen after Joki 1952: 108).

1969: VEWT: OTkc. buɣudaj < Mo. buɣudaj

1972: Clauson: OTkc. buğdāj, buğdaj

1972: Dmitrieva: only indicates a comparison with OTkc. boguz 'хлеб в зерне; фураж', boj 'пажитник'

1974: ÈSTJa: summarizes and comments on other propositions without offering its own. It only proposes to assume the possibility of final -g instead of -j, however, basing solely on Uzb.dial. forms buɣdaɣ ~ buɣdək. What seems to be more probable is an expansion of original *boguda (see ТКС. FORMS below) with a common suffix -(a)k on the Uzb. ground. Such an explanation is not in contradiction to the commonness of final -j in almost all Tkc. languages – which suggests a very old derivation – as -a forms appear quite often in dialects, especially in the Az. and Tksh. ones (cf. e.g. Tksh.dial. bağda ÈSTJa; boğda AA, RA; byjda OA; Az.dial. boɣda, buɣda ÈSTJa) which leads us to believe that the non-deminutive (see ETYMOLOGY below) form must have been in use for quite a long period.

2000: Tatarincev: *bug/k (nominal or verbal) 'greater quantity; multiplication; spreading' for multiple grains on the ear + the -(α)d- suffix forming verbs > 'накапливаться, скапливаться (напр., о зернах в клосе)' + suffixes forming nouns -(a)j, -a and -(a)g.
     To support the reconstructed *bug ~ *buk the following examples are listed: Yak. buguj 'пододвигать с краев к середине горяще в костре дрова', OUyg. puklun 'накоплять', Lob. bug-ana(k) 'насыпанные, пригнанные ветром бугры песку около деревьев' and others, also Kzk. bukpa 'густая каша', OTkc. boɣuz 'хлеб в зерне; фураж', Uyg. bogaz (in aš bogaz), boguz ~ bogus 'провиант для людей; корм для скота', and finally Tkc. bug ~ bugu 'пар, испарения, дым' and such coincidences as Kklp. buvdaj 'wheat' : buv 'steam' &c., and others.
     This proposition does not seem to be particularly convincing. The reconstruction of *bug/k with the above meaning is perhaps not so well grounded. Also the question of alternating o ~ u in the first syllable remains unsolved, particularly as it would be very hard to explain it by using the assumption of the original *u. Also the explanation of the differences in the auslaut of the Tkc. forms appears too brief.

2002: Tietze: < OTkc. buɣdaj (according to Clauson 1972)

Čuv. *pări*:

1946: Räsänen: 25f.: = Tkc. bugdaj

1973: Brands: 45: = Tkc. bugdaj

1977: Scherner: 17: late Bulgh. *buraj < early Bulgh. *buzaj < Tkc. *buɣδaj 'wheat'

1990: Róna-Tas: 31: Čuv.Virjal pŏri, Anatri pări < OTkc. buɣdaj; meaning influenced by Russ. pyrej 'spelt'.
     Róna-Tas assumes a disappearance of γ, spirantization of d > z, the Chuvash rhotacism and later, a reduction of u, yielding finally pŏri in Virjal and pări in Anatri. An explanation of the phonetic evolution of the last syllable is somewhat missing.

It might be impossible to present any proof, for or against, such an evolution. We believe however that Fedotov's proposition is more realistic because it assumes less phonetic changes, and the ones it includes are easier to explain, and involves no semantic change at all.

1996: Fedotov: < OSlav. *pyro* 'spelt'

Criticises connecting the word with Tkc. *bugdaj*, as has been done in the past. Instead, he offers a comparison with OSlav. *pyro* 'spelt', which seems quite convincing – both from the semantic and phonetic points of view (although the final -*i* still remains incomprehensible: an influence/contamination with *pyrej* 'spelt'?). A long-lasting and very thorough influence of Russ. on Čuv. is another argument in favour of Fedotov's 1996 proposition, even though he does not mention it himself.

COMMENTARY:

This word is very common in the Tkc. languages and, as one would expect, it appears in a multitude of phonetic shapes. It is also present in the Mo. languages, its forms being equally diversified there. In addition, we know that wheat is generally one of the oldest, or perhaps the oldest, cereal cultivated by man (Nowiński 1970: 162). A combination of these facts allows us to assume that this word existed as early as the stage of the Tkc.Mo. union (of whatever nature it was: genetic, areal or something else) or even earlier.[55] Unfortunately, our knowledge is not deep enough to try to produce an acceptably probable reconstruction on a stage of evolution that was so long before the oldest texts. This is why we are going to limit ourselves to offering some remarks on previous propositions, and presenting some possibilities for future investigation.

TKC. FORMS

Many of the Tkc. forms could be comfortably explained by a borrowing from another Tkc. language. This phenomenon has been and still is, quite common; in the past it was additionally facilitated by the nomadic way of life of many Tkc. tribes. An exact investigation into the routes of such borrowings is only possible to a very limited degree due to the poor and young attestations of many languages, and the orthographical tradition of literary koines, almost always very strong.

However, even without knowing precisely what the routes of our word are, it is possible to explain a great majority of its forms with just a few phonetic processes:
- spirantization and disappearance of -*g*-, along with possible substitute lengthening of the preceding vowel and possibly, its shortening later
- change of -*g*- > -*v*- or -*j*-, and

---

55 Its absence from the Ma.Tung. languages seems to indicate some transitional period between the Tkc.Mo.-Tung. and Tkc.Mo. unions. It is not, however, a very sound argument: all these peoples mainly made their living from nomadism well into historic times, and only regarded farming as an additional source of food for a very long time. Agricultural terms then, did not not necessarily spread fast and reach all the languages.

An attempt to ascertain whether the Ma.Tung. peoples were powerful enough to possess lands adequate for wheat cultivation would require an assumption of when our word is present in the Alt. languages, and would thus lead to a vicious circle.

- palatalization of a before *j* are all common phenomena in the Tkc. languages.
Individual forms in some of the languages might raise doubts but most of them can
be explained quite easily.
- Brb., Khak., Oyr., Sal. and Tuv. forms have initial *p-* instead of *b-*. In Khak. and Sal. it
is a regular change but it is not in the remaining languages. We believe that borrowing
is the most likely solution – perhaps from Khak., given the area of its usage.
- Čag., CTat., Kar., OTkc., Ott. and Trkm. *budɣaj* are most probably the result of
a metathesis.
- Kklp., Kzk. and Nog. *-i-* in the first syllable might be understood as a result of an
irregular process present in a part of the Tkc. languages where the dropping of
a consonant is accompanied by the change of the preceding vowel into ī.
- Tat. and Bšk. *böraj* are most probably borrowings from Čuv. (Fedotov 1996 s.v. *pări*).
Also Bšk. *buraj* can presumably be interpreted in this way. Still, a direct influence
of Russ. *pyrej* 'spelt' should not be ruled out, either.
- Tat. and Bšk. *-ö-* in the first syllable probably results from the influence (contamination?) of the form *böraj* which has been borrowed from Čuv. (see below).
- Uyg. three syllable long *buɣudaj* is presumably a borrowing from Mo. It is very unlikely that Uyg. would conserve the original (see below) high vowel in the middle
syllable of a three syllable word.

It seems then, that a great number of Tkc. forms (not counting Čuv. forms (see below)
and borrowings such as Uyg. *buɣudaj*) can in fact be reduced to one initial shape of
*boɣuda, because:
- Tkc. languages generally tend to avoid *o* in the first syllable, and so raising the
original *o* is much more likely than the opposite process
- Tkc. languages generally shorten three syllable words with a high vowel in the
middle syllable, while the Mo. languages do not (at least until quite recently)
- final *-j* is probably a diminutive suffix. This assumption has already been made
(e.g. ÈSTJa, Tatarincev 2000 and others), as it allows for an easy explanation of the
-a ~ *-aj* alternation in auslaut. For auslaut cf. also commentary on ÈSTJa's proposition in ETYMOLOGY above, and Tuv. *arbaj*, *arvaj*
For Čuv. *pări*, we believe, Fedotov's 1996 proposition (see ETYMOLOGY above) is the
most probable. If it is, however, true, it makes deriving Hung. *búza* 'wheat' from Čuv.
(TESz, EWU) impossible.

PTkc.Mo. NATIVENESS
None of the propositions for explaining our word on the Tkc. ground which have
been made so far is fully convincing. Tatarincev 2000 has certainly presented the
most probable proposition, though even this has a number of weak points: especially
semantics and connecting the word finally with 'steam' seems to be a little too far-
reaching. Also, as Tatarincev himself admits, the morphological structure is not fully
explained, either.

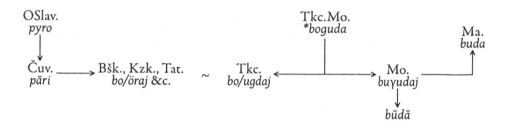

The Tkc. final -*aj* (though other forms exist, too) could have influenced Bšk., Kzk. and Tat. form borrowed from Čuv. We believe that this is more probable than trying to derive the word directly from the Čuv. form.

Borrowing to PTkc.Mo.

Perhaps then, we should look for the source of our word beyond the Tkc. and Mo. languages. The Chin. proposition in Joki 1952 is unacceptable for phonetic reasons (ÈSTJa, Tatarincev 2000). While an IE origin is probable for the Čuv. word (< Russ.), it is highly unlikely for all the remaining Tkc. languages, again, for phonetic reasons (PIE or IE -*r*- could not have yielded Tkc.Mo. -*γd*-).

We believe that the facts that, 1. the cultivation of wheat began in Mesopotamia, and 2. agriculture (together with the first cultivated cereals) seems to be a borrowing among the Tkc. (and Mo.) peoples, allows us to assume with equal probability that the name for 'wheat' was borrowed along with the plant itself, or that it was formed on the PTkc. or Mo. ground.

Currently, the situation appears to be a stalemate and allows for nothing but guesswork. We believe, nevertheless, that the lack of a convincing native explanation, and the incomprehensible morphological structure indicate a foreign origin, even if no probable etymon can be presented at the moment.

Nostratic

Gamkrelidze-Ivanov 1984 see the possibility of connecting the Tkc. and Mo. forms with PIE **pūròs*, Hung. *búza* and NPers. *buza* 'wheat'. As Witczak 2003: 95 has rightly remarked, however, this comparison is mainly based on their phonetic similarity, and should be considered wrong.[56] The forms which he proceeds to list later show clearly the extremes such comparisons could lead to: Arab. *burr* 'wheat', Fi. *puuro* 'groats, grits', Melan. *pura* 'fruit', Polyn. *pura-pura* 'grain' and others.

Finally, we would like to mention a word which is not very often mentioned in this context: Tkc. *buza* 'wheat beer'[57] and perhaps Slav. and other *braga* 'various types of

---

56 Witczak 2003: 96 also provides further bibliography of negative opinions on this proposition.

57 Also Hung.dial. *boza* 'alcohol beverage made of cereal, similar to beer', which however, is most probably a borrowing from Tkc. (Čuv.?).

alcohol beverages'[58]. The connection with *bugdaj*, even if self-evident to some extent, is very difficult to thoroughly establish, at least in the case of *buza*, and requires further investigation, presumably reaching far beyond Turkology[59] – like the ultimate etymology of *bugdaj* itself.

DÖVME

FORMS: *dövme* **Tksh.**: Eren 1999 'husked wheat; and others'
ETYMOLOGY: 1999: Eren: < *döv-* 'to beat, to hit'
COMMENTARY: This word is absolutely clear. Cf. also *tögü* 'millet', *tüvi* 'rice'.

DÜGI

FORMS: *dügi* **Tat.**: دوگی Tanievъ 1909
ETYMOLOGY: see *tüvi* 'rice'
COMMENTARY:

In Tat. this word appears also as *döge* and *dŏgŏ*, and meaning 'rice'. Generally, the word originates ultimately from **tög-* ~ **töv-* 'to beat, to hit' and is common in the Tkc. languages with the meanings of 'rice' and 'millet'; 'wheat' might then come as a surprise. We believe it might turn out to be an interesting confirmation of our proposition on the two-fold origin of modern forms (see *tüvi* 'rice'). We can see in theory four possibilities of explaining this form:

1. < **tög-i* (while *döge*, *dŏgŏ* < **tög-e*).

    If we accept the view of the original two-fold derivation, we may believe that both forms have been conserved in Tat., and that their meanings diversified in the following way: the old -*ö* derivative preserved the most common, and probably the original meaning, 'rice', and the -*i* derivative gained a new one, 'wheat'. It might be viewed as surprising, however, that it is 'wheat' and not 'millet', the former being the second most common meaning of our word in the Tkc. languages (see *tögü* 'millet'). We suppose this could have resulted from the fact that wheat has always been one of the most, or even the most important cereal – not only for the Turks, but for a considerable part of Eurasia.

    Such an explanation seems to be reasonably plausible, probably more so than the others.

---

58 Scherner 1977: 17: Russ. *brága* 'type of weak beer (Dünnbier)' < MČuv. **bura* + -*ka* (Vga), which is however, not very convincing due to Russ. accent not on the last syllable.
    Presumably, the IE counterparts, especially Celt. (cf. e.g. Černych 1993, Vasmer 1986–87) indicate an IE origin of this word. We believe that if the connection with the Tkc. forms exists at all, than the direction of influence is just opposite to the one proposed by Scherner 1977: 17.

59 Cf. Tietze 2000, where Tksh. *boza* 'weak alcohol beverage made of millet' is derived from Pers. *būza* 'millet' (cf. however Rubinčik 1970, where بزا، بزه *buza*, *buze* exclusively in meaning 'millet beer' and بوز *bouz* 'mould, fungus' and بیزك *bouzak* 'yeast, sourdough'), and where a further bibliography can be found.

2. 'rice' > 'wheat'.

    One could assume that this change is a later innovation in Tat. It could be explained then by the fact that after the Tatars departed westwards, away from the influence of the Chin. culture, they moved onto an area where the Pers. culture was dominant. For the Persians, wheat was the primary cereal. However, in Persia rice was known and popular, too: four out of nine names for 'rice' in the Tkc. languages, whose etymology is acceptable, are of Pers. origin. Moreover, this proposition does not explain the difference in sounding between *dügi* and *döge, dŏgŏ*.

3. It cannot be completely discounted that our word was borrowed from some other language. This, however, hardly explains its non-standard meaning.

4. Some kind of unification or mixing of 'rice' and 'wheat', such as e.g. 'millet' and 'corn' (see *mysyr* 'millet' where further references can be found), or 'oats' and 'barley' (see *julaf* 'oats' where further references can be found). This possibility is, however, not very likely as it would be the only example of such a phenomenon involving these two cereals.

GENIM

FORMS: *genim* **Tksh.dial.:** Bläsing 1995: 25
ETYMOLOGY: 1995: Bläsing: 25: < Zaza *genim*
COMMENTARY: Bläsing's 1995 etymology appears to be irrefutable.

GÖŽE

FORMS: *göže* **Tksh.:** ÈSTJa 'husked wheat'
ETYMOLOGY: see *köče* 'barley'
COMMENTARY:

The only semantic parallel we know of is *aš(lyk)* (cf. *as* 'barley', *aš(lyk)* 'wheat'), combining in one word the meanings of 'barley' and 'wheat'.

HINTA

FORMS: *hinta* **Ott.:** حنطه Wiesentahl 1895, Redhouse 1921
ETYMOLOGY: as yet not discussed
COMMENTARY: < Arab. حنطه *hinṭa* 'wheat'.

JASMYK

FORMS: *jasmyk* **Uzb.dial.:** ÈSTJa 'species of wheat'
ETYMOLOGY: see *jasymuk* 'millet'
COMMENTARY:

While this word is absolutely clear morphologically, its meaning of 'wheat' is enigmatic. When taking into consideration the original meaning of this word, *?'something flat'[60] (> 'lentil', also 'millet'), one can only guess that one of the species of wheat has characteristically flatter grains, or perhaps some similarity to 'millet'.

KYZYL BODAJ

FORMS: *kyzyl bodaj* **Tat.:** Voskresenskij 1894 'wheat (with red grains)'
ETYMOLOGY: as yet not discussed
COMMENTARY:
   This word is absolutely clear: *kyzyl* 'red' (from the colour of grains) + *bodaj* 'wheat'.

KYZYLTAS

FORMS: *kyzyl tas* **Tuv.:** Dmitrieva 1972 || *kyzyltas* RTuwS
ETYMOLOGY: 1972: Dmitrieva: < *kyzyl* 'red' + *tas* 'bald; naked; with scarce vegetation'
COMMENTARY:
   This word may be more complex than has been presented by Dmitrieva 1972. While the first part of her etymology seems to be highly plausible (cf. *kyzyl bodaj*), its second element and the type of the compound are rather odd: 1. it is unclear why 'wheat' should be described as 'bald, naked'; perhaps the word in fact means not 'wheat' but just one of the species, which could be characterised as such? 2. to the best of our knowledge, in the Tkc. languages there are no compounds with a nominal meaning, which would be made up of two adjectives[61]. Unfortunately, the second part[62] of this word remains puzzling for us, too.

MEJZƏ

FORMS: *mejzə* **Fuyü:** Zhen-hua 1987
ETYMOLOGY: as yet not discussed
COMMENTARY: < Mand. *maɪ⁴zi* 'wheat' (oral information from Prof. A. Vovin [Honolulu]).

ÖJÜR

FORMS: *öjür* **OTkc.:** Egorov 1964, Fedeotov 1996 'millet; spelt'
ETYMOLOGY: see *ügür* 'millet'
COMMENTARY:
   The etymology of this word has not been fully ascertained. However, from the original meaning of 'gruel, pap', a semantic evolution to any cereal is possible. Given that wheat

---

60 This meaning is most probably, though not definitely, simply a methodological support.

61 Although this distinction can hardly ever be justified for the Tkc. languages, in this very case the adjectival nature of 'red' and 'bald' on one hand, and the nominal of 'wheat' on the other is exceptionally explicit.

62 It cannot be discounted that the word is not in fact a compound but a borrowing whose sounding is by chance (or perhaps as a result of contamination or adaptation?) identical to that of *kyzyl* 'red'.

has always been one of the, or even the most important cereal, it might seem odd that this word has mainly survived in the meaning of 'millet', but not 'wheat'. Cf. *taryg*.

SELIEHINEJ

FORMS:
seliehinej **Yak.**: RJakS
seliesenej, seliesinej **Yak**: [ɔ: -ehe/i-] Pekarskij 1917–30, Dmitrieva 1972, Anikin 2003
ETYMOLOGY:
    1964:　Slepcov: 91: < Russ. *pšeničnyj* 'wheat [adj.]'
    1972:　Dmitrieva: < Russ. *silosnyj* 'silo [adj.]'
    2003:　Anikin 2003: < Russ.dial. *pšenίčnoj (-yj)* 'wheat [adj.]' = Russ. liter. *pšeničnyj* id.
COMMENTARY:

The etymology proposed by Slepcov 1964: 91 is much more probable on the semantic side. Phonetically, Russ. *n* happens to yield *l* in Yak., as in e.g. *Alampažɣs* < Russ. *Anemlodist*, Yak. *balakažɣla* < Russ. *panikadilo* (Slepcov 1964: 91). Anikin 2003 additionally allows the possibility of simplification *pš-* > *š-* still on the Russ. ground, which indeed cannot be ruled out, but also in all likelihood cannot be proved.

    The etymology offered by Dmitrieva 1972 is not only very unlikely semantically, it also raises doubts about its phonetic nature: it is not absolutely clear why Russ. *í-o-y* or even *i-ó-y*[63] should yield *e-ie-e* in Yak.

ŠENĪSE

FORMS: *šenīse, šīse* **Tof.**: RTofS, Anikin 2003 || *šīse* Rassadin 1971: 231, Anikin 2003
ETYMOLOGY:
    1971:　Rassadin: 231: *šise* < Bur. *šenīse* < Russ. *pšenica*
    2003:　Anikin: ? *šīse, šīse* < Russ. *pšenica*
          šenīse < Bur. *šenīse* < Russ. *pšenica* (after Rassadin 1971)
COMMENTARY:

It is difficult to find a major weakness in the etymology proposed by Rassadin 1971: 23. The expression in Anikin 2003 is not fully clear: it gives the impression that he wants to derive *šīse, šīse* directly from Russ. without the Bur. mediation, which seems to be less likely. We believe that Russ. *pšenica* > Bur. *šenīse* > Tof. *šenīse* > *šīse* > *šīse*.

TARYG

FORMS: *taryg* **MTkc.MK**: Dankoff/Kelly 1982–85
ETYMOLOGY:　see *dary* 'millet'

---

63 There also exists, though it is considered to be incorrect, the form *silósnyj*, see Ageenko 2001: '*sílosnyj*, not *silósnyj*'.

COMMENTARY:

This word is very common in the Tkc. languages, but generally signifies 'millet'. The reconstruction of its original shape and meaning **tar-yg* '(what was) sowed' raises no serious doubts. For the meaning of 'wheat' cf. *öjür*.

TEREKE

FORMS: *tereke* **Gag.**: Özkan 1996
ETYMOLOGY: see *darikan* 'rye'
COMMENTARY:

This name is ultimately of Arm. origin, and most probably came to Gag. through one of the Tksh. dialects, together with settlers from Anatolia, who were displaced onto the conquered territories in the Ottoman Empire. This word, sounding *tereke* existed in Ott. between the 14th and 18th centuries meaning 'harvest; cereal' (Dankoff 1995: 702), from where a shift to 'wheat' is trivial, given great importance of this cereal in the region.

Cf. *darikan* 'rye'.

TULA

FORMS:

tula **Čuv.**: Dmitrieva 1972
tulă **Čuv.**: Nikolьskij 1909, RČuvS-D, RČuvS-E ‖ (*sară*) *tulă*, RČuvS-A

ETYMOLOGY:

1972: Dmitrieva: < Georg. *doli* 'husked wheat', *dola* 'bread of husked wheat' (after: Abaev, I 400), at the same time indicating a comparison to Mo. *talx(an)* 'хлеб печеный', Bur. *talx(an)* 'flour; dough; хлеб', Ir. **talxan* 'жареные и молотые зерна бобовых'

COMMENTARY:

The etymology proposed by Dmitrieva 1972 does not seem to be totally unrealistic, although it does have several weaknesses. It tacitly assumes a Georg. influence on Čuv. which is possible but unlikely, especially in the case of the name for 'wheat' which the Turks had presumably already known well; and thus borrowing it from Georgians – a nation of highlanders, not known for their farming – would be strange. Cf. *nartük* 'corn', in this case, though, the geographical distribution (Krč.Blk. and Nog.) definitely makes this kind of borrowing much more likely.

We would like to mention that in theory this word could also be identified with *sula* &c. 'oats' by means of a quite common but not described, and thus unpredictable alternation *s : t*. However, this is perhaps not very probable as it would be the only example of combining in one word the meanings of 'wheat' and 'oats'.

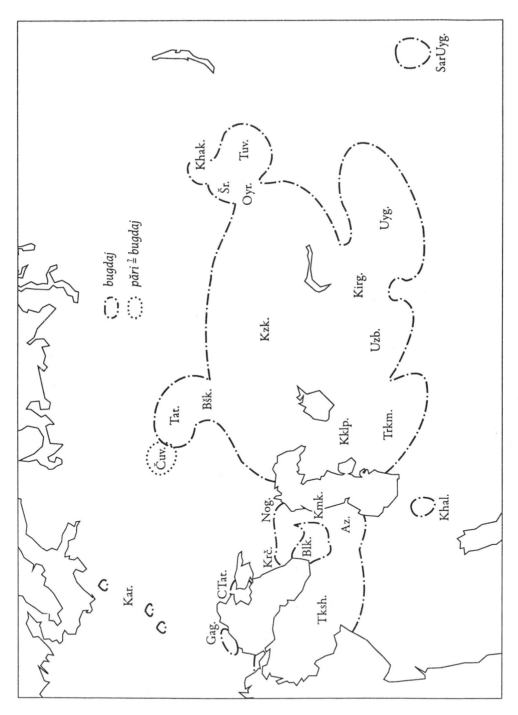

Legend:
—·—·— *bugdaj*
········· *pări* [2] *bugdaj*

Map labels: SarUyg., Khak., Tuv., Šr., Oyr., Uyg., Kirg., Kzk., Uzb., Bšk., Tat., Čuv., Kklp., Trkm., Khal., Kmk., Nog., Az., Krč., Blk., Kar., CTat., Gag., Tksh.

bugdaj 'wheat'

STATISTICS

The table below shows the number of words (not entries) dealt with in this work. The following rules have been observed during its preparation:

– words which are eventually the same but appear in different meanings (e.g. *dary* Tkc. 'millet', Tksh.dial. 'corn') were counted as one
– compounds and abbreviations were counted as one: e.g. *mysyr* (< Arab.; an abbreviation of *mysyr bugdajy*) and *mysyr bugdajy* (< ?), were both counted as one native word with an acceptable etymology, since the compound has most probably been created on the Tkc. ground
– one word borrowed in different morphological forms, or adapted phonetically in different ways (e.g. Bšk. *ovsa*, Tof. *ovjot*, Trkm. *ovjos* 'oats') was counted as one

The overall number of words counted according to the above rules is 86. However, for ease of usage they have been divided into 106 entries.

cereal	etymology	Tkc.	< Arab.	< Chin.	< Pers.	< Russ.	< other	overall
barley	acceptable	2	1			2	2	7
	dubious	1						1
	unknown							2
corn	acceptable	12				1	1	14
	dubious							
	unknown							2
oats	acceptable	6				2		8
	dubious							
	unknown							4
millet	acceptable	8		1	2	1		12
	dubious	2						2
	unknown							2
wheat	acceptable	3	1	1		2	2	9
	dubious	1						1
	unknown							2
rice	acceptable	3			4		2	9
	dubious							
	unknown							2

cereal	etymology	Tkc.	< Arab.	< Chin.	< Pers.	< Russ.	< other	overall
rye	acceptable	5		1	2			8
	dubious	1						1
	unknown							
overall	acceptable	39	2	2	7	10	7	67
	dubious	5						5
	unknown							14
	overall	44	2	2	7	10	7	86

Most common naming patterns

Almost a half of the words discussed here are borrowings, and thus cannot be taken into consideration when describing the Tkc. naming patterns. Most of the native words, however, are not built on the basis of any repetitive pattern. In fact, merely two general patterns can be clearly distinguished, and they both have a fairly limited geographic and/or semantic range:

1. attribute + 'cereal'. name of a cereal or something similar
   Ten names are built according to this pattern, which can be divided into two, partly overlapping subgroups:
   a) the attribute is a colour name
      - *kara*: *kara bugdaj* 'rye' in various languages of Central Asia
      - *ak*: Tuv. *akbydā*, Tof. *ak h(ü)rüpē* 'rice'; Tuv. *aktarā* 'wheat'
      - *kök*: Kzk. *kök najza*, Tuv. *kök tarā* 'rye'
   b) the second part is *tarā* '1. cereal; 2. millet'
   Tuv. *aktarā* 'wheat', *a"tarāzy* 'oats', *čingetarā* 'millet', *köktarā* 'rye', *xōtarā* 'millet'
2. place name + name of a cereal
   This patterns only appears with the names for 'corn':
   - Tat. *käbä bödoj*
   - Kklp. *mäkke* (abbreviation of a compound), Kirg., Kklp., Uyg., Uzb. *meke žügörü* Trkm. *mekgežöven*
   - Tksh. *mysyr* (*bugdajy*)
   - Ott. *šam darysy*
3. derived from 'to hit, to strike'
   dövme || *dügi* || *öjür*
4. derived from 'to bury, to dig'
   kömme qonaq || *sokpa*
5. borrowed from an oblique case
   Most probably these are forms of Gen.Sg., presumably used in the function of Part. There are exclusively borrowings from Russ. here.
   ovsa || *prosa* || *rži*

SEMANTIC TYPES

Three, partly overlapping semantic types can be spotted:

1. names meaning exactly one cereal

    This is the dominant type. There are borrowings, compounds and rare native names here, e.g. *ebies* 'oats', *pirinč* 'rice', *ša'ïr* 'barley', *tereke* 'rye'; *mekgežöven* 'corn'; *sary* 'corn' and others.

2. names, the etymology of which allows for diverse semantic development

    For obvious reasons, there are native names only in this group: *aš(lyk)* 'barley; wheat', *bordoq* 'corn; oats', *dary* 'corn; millet', *dügi* 'millet; rice', *jasmyk* 'corn; millet' and *öjür* 'corn; millet; wheat'.

    Perhaps also *arpagan* 'barley; oats' could be considered a member of this group, too. Words which belong to this type, mostly belong to type 3. as well.

3. names which can mean different cereals in a non-chaotic way

    a) 'barley' > 'oats'

        arpa ‖ *arpagan* ‖ *julaf* ‖ *sula*[64] ‖ *taɣ arpasy*

    b) 'barley' and 'wheat'

        aš(łyk) ‖ *köže*

    c) 'millet' > 'corn'

        basadohan ‖ *čüžgün*[65] ‖ *dary* ‖ *jasmyk* ‖ *öjür* ‖ *šam darysy*

    d) 'rice' and 'rye'

        aryš ‖ *suly*

---

64 *Sula* is the only name here, which developed in the opposite direction, i.e. 'oats' > 'barley'.

65 In the case of *čüžgün* the direction of the development remains unknown. Surely, Uyghurs became acquainted with corn later than millet but we do not know for how long this word has existed in Uyg., and what its original meaning was.

Afgh. = Afghan || **Alb.** = Albanian || **Alt.** = Altaic || **Arab.** = Arabic || **Arm.** = Armenian || **AS** = Anglo-Saxon || **Av.** = Avestan || **Az.** = Azerbaijanian || **Blk.** = Balkar || **Blr.** = Belorussian || **Bosn.Tksh.** = Bosnian Turkish || **Brb.** = Baraba || **Bšk.** = Bashkir || **Bulg.** = Bulgarian (Slavic) || **Bur.** = Buryat || **Cauc.** = Caucasian || **Celt.** = Celtic || **Chin.** = Chinese || **Com.** = Coman || **Crm.** = Crimean || **CTat.** = Crimean Tatar || **Cz.** = Czech || **Čag.** = Chagatai || **Čul.** = Chulym || **Čuv.** = Chuvash || **D.** = Dutch || **dial.** = dialectal || **Dolg.** = Dolgan || **E.** = East || **Eng.** = English || **Evk.** = Evenki || **Fi.** = Finnish || **Fr.** = French || **G.** = German || **Gag.** = Gagaus || **Georg.** = Georgian || **Gr.** = Greek || **Grmc.** = Germanic || **Hebr.** = Hebrew || **Hung.** = Hungarian || **IE** = Indo-European || **Ir.** = Iranian || **It.** = Italian || **Jap.** = Japanese || **Kar.** = Karaim || **KarC** = Karaim of Crimea || **KarH** = Karaim of Halych || **KarL** = Karaim of Luck || **KarT** = Karaim of Trakai || **Khak.** = Khakas || **Khal.** = Khalaj || **Kipč.** = Kipchak || **Kirg.** = Kirghiz || **Kklp.** = Karakalpak || **Klmk.** = Kalmuk || **Kmk.** = Kumyck || **Kmnd.** = Kumandin || **KorS** = South Korean || **Koyb.** = Koybal || **Krč.** = Karachay || **Krč.Blk.** = Karachay-Balkar || **Küär.** = Küärik || **Kurd.** = Kurdish || **Kzk.** = Kazakh || **Lat.** = Latin || **Leb.** = Lebedin || **liter.** = literary || **Lith.** = Lithuanian || **Lob.** = Lobnor || **LSorb.** = Lower Sorbian || **Ma.** = Manchu || **Mand.** = Mandarin || **MBšk.** = Middle Bashkir || **MChin.** = Middle Chinese || **Melan.** = Melanesian || **MIr.** = Middle Iranian || **MMo.** = Middle Mongolian || **Mo.** = Mongol || **MPers.** = Middle Persian || **MTat.** = Middle Tatar || **MTkc.** = Middle Turkic || **MTkc.H** = Houtsma 1894 || **MTkc.IM** = Battal 1934 || **MTkc.KD** = Golden 2000 || **MTkc.MA** = MTkc. in *Muqaddimat al-'Adab* || **MTkc.MA.B** = Borovkov 1971 || **MTkc.MK** = MTkc. in the Mahmud al-Kashgari's dictionary || **N.** = North || **Nan.** = Nanai || **Nog.** = Nogai || **NPers.** = New Persian || **OBask.** = Old Basque || **OChin.** = Old Chinese || **OČuv.** = Old Chuvash || **OESlav.** = Old East Slavic || **Oghuz.** = Oghuzic || **Oghuz.Ir.** = Oghuzic in Iran || **OInd.** = Old Indian || **OIr.** = Old Iranian || **OJap.** = Old Japanese || **OKipč.** = Old Kipchak || **ORuss.** = Old Russian || **OSlav.** = Old Slavonic || **Osset.** = Ossetic || **OTkc.** = Old Turkic || **Ott.** = Ottoman || **OUyg.** = Old Uyghur || **OVanj.** = Old Vanjan || **Oyr.** = Oyrot || **Paleo-Europ.** = Paleo-European || **PAlt.** = Proto-Altaic || **Pamir.** = Pamirian || **Pers.** = Persian || **PIE** = Proto-Indo-European || **Pol.** = Polish || **Polyn.** = Polynesian || **Russ.** = Russian || **S.** = South || **Sag.** = Sagal || **Sal.** = Salar || **SarUyg** = Sary-Uyghur || **SC** = Serbo-Croatian || **Serb.** = Serbian || **Sib.** = Siberian || **Skr.** = Sanskrit || **Slav.** = Slavonic || **Slvk.** = Slovak || **Slvn.** = Slovenian || **Sol.** = Solon || **Sp.** = Spanish || **Šr.** = Šor || **Taj.** = Tajik || **Tat.** = Tatar || **Tat.Gr.** = Podolsky 1981 || **Tel.** = Teleut || **Tkc.** = Turkic || **Tkc.Mo.** = Turkic-Mongolian || **Tksh.** = Turkish || **Tob.** = Tobol || **Toch.** = Tocharian || **Tof.** = Tofalar || **Trkm.** = Turkmen || **Tung.** = Tungusic || **Tuv.** = Tuvinian || **Ukr.** = Ukrainian || **Ulč.** = Ulča-Tungusic || **USorb.** = Upper Sorbian || **Uyg.** = Uyghur || **Uzb.** = Uzbek || **VBulgh.2** = Volga-Bulgharian || **W.** = West || **WMo.** = Written Mongolian || **Xlx.** = Khalkha || **Yak.** = Yakut || **Yazg.** = Yazghulami

LITERATURE

AA = Nakib, B.: *Antakya Ağzı. Dilbilgisi ve Sözlük*, Antakya 2004

Abaev, V.I.: *Istoriko-ètimologičeskij slovarъ osetinskogo jazyka*, Moskva–Leningrad 1958–89

Achmetъjanov, R.G.: *Obščaja leksika materialьnoj kulьtury narodov srednego Povolžьja*, Moskva 1989

Adjagaši [= Agyagási], K.: *Rannie russkie zaimstvovanija tjurkiskich jazykov volgo-kamskogo areala* I (= Studies in Linguistics of the Volga-Region 2), Szeged 2005

Ageenko, F.L.: *Sobstvennye imena v russkom jazyke. Slovarъ udarenij*, Moskva 2001

Alijiv, A. / Böörijif, K.: *Orysča-turkmenče sözlik*, 1929

AMA = Boz, E.: *Afyon Merkez Ağzı*, Afyon 2002

Anikin, A.E.: *Ètimologičeskij slovarъ russkich dialektov Sibiri. Zaimstvovanija iz uralьskich, altajskich i paleoaziatskich jazykov*, Novosibirsk 1998

Anikin, A.E.: *Ètimologičeskij slovarъ russkich zaimstvovanij v jazykach Sibiri*, Novosibirsk 2003

AOH = *Acta Orientalia Academiae Scientiarum Hungaricae*, Budapest

Ašmarin, N.L.: *Thesaurus linguae Tschuvaschorum*, Kazanъ (some volumes Čeboksary) 1928–50

Bańkowski, A.: *Etymologiczny słownik języka polskiego*, Warszawa 2000–

Barchudarov, S.G. et al. (eds.): *Slovarъ russkogo jazyka XI-XVII vv.*, Moskva 1975–

Battal, A.: *İbnü-Mühennâ Lügati*, İstanbul 1934

Baxter, W.: *An Etymological Dictionary of Common Chinese Characters* [draft 28.10.2000], http://www-personal.umich.edu/~wbaxter/etymdict.html

Benzing, J.: Die angeblichen bolgartürkischen Lehnwörter im Ungarischen. – *ZDMG* 98 (N.F. 23) 1 (1944): 24–27

Benzing, J.: *Die tungusischen Sprachen. Versuch einer vergleichenden Grammatik* (= Akademie der Wissenschaften und der Literatur. Abhandlungen der geistes- und sozialwissen- schaftlichen Klasse Nr. 11), Wiesbaden 1955

BER = Georgiev, V. et al. (eds.): *Bъlgarski etimologičen rečnik*, Sofija 1971–

Berneker, E.: *Slavisches etymologisches Wörterbuch. A–morъ*, Heidelberg 1908–13

Bläsing, U.: *Armenisches Lehngut im Türkeitürkischen am Beispiel von Hemşin*, Amsterdam– Atlanta 1992

Bläsing, U.: Kurdische und Zaza-Elemente im türkeitürkischen Dialektlexicon. – *DS-NELL* 2 (1995): 173–218

Borovkov, A.K.: Nazvanija rastenij po bucharskomu spisku „Mukaddimat al-adab". – Baska- kov, N.A. et al. (eds.): *Tjurkskaja leksikologija i leksikografija*, Moskva 1971: 96–111

Boryś, W.: *Słownik etymologiczny języka polskiego*, Kraków 2005

Brands, H.W.: *Studien zum Wortbestand der Türksprachen*, Leiden 1973

Brückner, A.: *Słownik etymologiczny języka polskiego*, Warszawa 1927

Cihac, A. de: *Dictionnaire d'étymologie daco-romane*, Francofort s/M 1879

Cincius, V.I.: *Sravnitelьnaja fonetika tunguso-manьčžurskich jazykov*, Leningrad 1949

Cioranescu, A.: *Diccionario etimológico rumano*, Tenerife 1966

Clauson, Sir G.: *An Etymological Dictionary of Pre-Thirteenth Century Turkish*, Oxford 1972

Černych, P.Ja.: *Istoriko-ètimologičeskij slovarь sovremennogo russkogo jazyka*, Moskva 1993

Çevilek, Ö.: *Dindışı Eski Uygurca Metinlerin Karşılaştırmalı Sözvarlığı*, İstanbul 2005 [unpublished MA thesis]

Dankoff, R.: *Armenian Loanwords in Turkish*, Wiesbaden 1995

Dankoff, R. / Kelly, J.: *Mahmūd al-Kāšγarī. Compendium of the Turkic Dialects (Dīwān Luγāt at-Turk)*, Harvard 1982–85

DFKzk = Kydyrbayeva, L.: *Dictionnaire français-kazakh*, Paris 1983

DKzkF = Indjoudjien, D.: *Dictionnaire kazakh-français*, Paris 1983

Dmitrieva, L.V.: Nazvanija rastenij v tjurkskich i drugich altajskich jazykach. – Cincius, V.I. (ed.): *Očerki sravnitelьnoj leksikologii altajskich jazykov*, Leningrad 1972: 151–223

Dmitrieva, L.V.: Iz ètimologii nazvanij rastenij v tjurkskich, mongolьskich i tungusomanьčžurskich jazykach. – Cincius, B.I. (ed.): *Issledovanija v oblasti ètimologii altajskich jazykov*, Leningrad 1979: 135–91

Doerfer, G.: *Lexik und Sprachgeographie des Chaladsch. Textband*, Wiesbaden 1987

Doerfer, G. / Hesche, W.: *Chorasantürkisch*, Wiesbaden 1993

Doerfer, G. / Hesche, W.: *Südoghusische Materialien aus Afghanistan und Iran*, Wiesbaden 1989

Doerfer, G. / Tezcan, S.: *Wörterbuch des Chaladsch (Dialekt von Xarrab)*, Budapest 1980

DS = *Derleme Sözlüğü*, Ankara 1993

DTS = Nadeljaev, V.M. / Nasilov, D.M. / Tenišev, È.R. / Ščerbak, A.M. (eds.): *Drevnetjurkskij slovarь*, Leningrad 1969

Dumézil, G.: *Légendes sur les Nartes suivies de cinq notes mythologiques* (= Bibliothèque de l'Institut français de Léningrad 11), Paris 1930

Egorov, V.G: *Ètimologičeskij slovarь čuvašskogo jazyka*, Čeboksary 1964

Erdal, M.: *Old Turkic Word Formation*, Wiesbaden 1991

Eren, H: *Türk Dilinin Etimolojik Sözlüğü*, Ankara 1999

ÈSTJa = Sevortjan, È.V. (ed.): *Ètimologičeskij slovarь tjurkskich jazykov*, Moskva 1974–

ESUM = Melьničuk, O.S. et al. (eds.): *Etimologičnij slovnik ukrajinskoji movi*, Kiïv 1982–

EVP = Morgenstierne, G.: *An Etymological Vocabulary of Pashto*, Oslo 1927

EWU = Benkő, L. et al. (eds.): *Etymologisches Wörterbuch des Ungarischen*, Budapest 1993–94

Fazylov, È.: *Starouzbekskij jazyk chorezmijskich pamjatnikov XIV veka*, Taškent 1966–71

Fedorov, A.I. (ed.): *Slovarь russkich govorov novosibirskoj oblasti*, Novosibirsk 1979

Fedotov, M.R.: *Ètimologičeskij slovarь čuvašskogo jazyka*, Čeboksary 1996

Filin, F.P. (ed.): *Slovarь russkich narodnych govorov*, Leningrad 1965–

FO = *Folia Orientalia*, Kraków

Frankle, E.: *Word Formation in the Turkic Languages*, Columbia 1948

FUF = *Finnisch-Ugrische Forschungen*, Helsinki

Gamkrelidze, T.V. / Ivanov, V.V.: *Indoevropejskij jazyk i indoevropejcy. Rekonstrukcija i istoriko-tipologičeskij analiz prajazyka i protokulьtury*, Tbilisi 1984

Genaust, H.: *Etymologisches Wörterbuch der botanischen Pflanzennamen*, Stuttgart 1976

Gluhak, A.: *Hrvatski etimološki rječnik*, Zagreb 1993

Golden, P.B. (ed.): *The King's Dictionary. The Rasûlid Hexaglot: Fourteenth Century Vocabularies in Arabic, Persian, Turkic, Greek, Armenian and Mongol*, Leiden–Boston–Köln 2000

Gombocz, Z.: *Die bulgarisch-türkischen Lehnwörter in der ungarischen Sprache*, Helsinki 1912

Grønbech, K.: *Komanisches Wörterbuch. Türkischer Wortindex zu Codex Cumanicus*, Kopenhagen 1942

Güngör, H. / Argunşah, M.: *Gagavuz Türkleri (Tarih – Dil – Folklor ve Halk Edebiyatı)*, Ankara 1991

Helimski [= Chelimskij], E.A.: Ètimologičeskie zametki. – Ulachanov, I.S. et al. (eds.): *Issledovanija po istoričeskoj grammatike i leksikologii*, Moskva 1990: 30–58

Helimski [= Chelimskij], E.A.: *Komparativistika, uralistika. Lekcii i statъi*, Moskva 2000

Holub, J. / Kopečný, F.: *Etymologický slovník jazyka českého*, Praha 1952

Holub, J. / Lyer, S.: *Stručný etymologický slovník jazyka českého*, Praha 1967

Horn, P.: *Grundriss der neupersischen Etymologie*, Strassburg 1893

Houtsma, M.Th.: *Ein türkisch-arabisches Glossar*, Leiden 1894

Hübschmann, H.: *Persische Studien*, Strassburg 1895

Hubschmid, J.: *Thesaurus Praeromanicus*. Faszikel 2, Bern 1965

Imanaevъ, M.: *Russko-tatarskij orfografičeskij slovarъ*, Kazanь 1901

Jarring, G.: *An Eastern Turki-English Dialect Dictionary*, Lund 1964

Jarring, G.: *Agriculture and Horticulture in Central Asia in Early Years of the Twentieth Century with an Excursus on Fishing*, Lund 1998

Joki, A.: *Die Lehnwörter des Sajan-Samojedischen*, Helsinki 1952

Jungmann, J.: *Slovník česko-německý*, Praha 1835–39

Kakuk, Zs.: Un vocabulaire salar. – *AOH* 14 (1962): 173–96

Kakuk, Zs.: *Mischärtatarische Texte mit Wörterverzeichnis*, Szeged 1996

Kannisto, A.: Die tatarischen Lehnwörter im Wogulischen. – *FUF* 17 (1925), Heft 1–3: 1–264

Karłowicz, J.: *Słownik wyrazów obcego a mniej jasnego pochodzenia używanych w języku polskim*, Kraków 1894–1905

Katanovъ, N.: *Kratkij russko-kirgizskij slovarъ*, Kazanь 1909

Kluge, F.: *Etymologisches Wörterbuch der deutschen Sprache*, Berlin–New York ²²1989

Kowalski, T: *Karaimische Texte im Dialekt von Troki* (= Prace Komisji Orjentalistycznej Polskiej Akademii Umiejętności 11), Kraków 1929

KRPS = Baskakov, N.A. / Zajączkowski, A. / Szapszał, S.M.: *Karaimsko-russko-polъskij slovarъ*, Moskva 1974

KSz = *Keleti Szemle*, Budapest

KTLCS = Ercilasun, A.B. / Aliyev, A.M.: *Karşılaştırmalı Türk Lehçeleri Cep Sözlüğü, 1: Türkiye Türkçesi / Azerbaycan Türkçesi, Azerbaycan Türkçesi / Türkiye Türkçesi*, Ankara 1991

KWb = Ramstedt, G.J.: *Kalmückisches Wörterbuch*, Helsinki 1935

Lapinъ, S.A.: *Russko-uzbekskij slovarъ*, Samarkandъ ²1899

Laude-Cirtautas, I.: *Das Gebrauch der Farbbezeichnungen in den Türkdialekten*, Wiesbaden 1961

Laufer, B.: *Sino-Iranica*, Chicago 1919

Levi, B.Z.: *Russko-karaimskij slovarъ. Krymskij dialekt*, Odessa 1996

Lidell, G.H.: *A Greek English Lexicon*, Oxford ⁹1968

Ligeti, L.: Histoire du lexique des langues turques. – *RO* 17 (1951–52): 80–91

Lokotsch, K.: *Etymologisches Wörterbuch der amerikanischen (indianischen) Wörter im Deutschen*, Heidelberg 1926

Lokotsch, K.: *Etymologisches Wörterbuch der europäischen (germanischen, romanischen und slavischen) Wörter orientalischen Ursprungs*, Heidelberg 1927

Lőrinczy, É. (ed.): *Új magyar tájszótár*, Budapest 1979–

Machek, V.: *Etymologický slovník jazyka českého*, Praha 1968

Maciuszak, K.: Persian checkmate – 'The King is oppressed'. On the origin of the chessmens' names. – *SEC* 8 (2003): 91–101

Mańczak, W.: Étymologie du français *sarrasin*. – *SEC* 4 (1999): 95–96

Mardkowicz, A.: *Karaj sez-bitigi. Słownik karaimski. Karaimisches Wörterbuch*, Łuck 1935

Martin, S.E.: *The Japanese Language Through Time*, New Haven–London 1987

Martynaŭ, V.U. (ed.): *Ètymalagičny sloŭnik belaruskaj movy*, Minsk 1978–

Mašanovъ, M.: *Russko-kirgizskij slovarъ*, Orenburg 1899

Maъrufov, È.M. (ed.): *Ūzbek tilining izoχli luγati*, Moskva 1981

Menges, K. (ed.): *Volkskundliche Texte aus Ost-Türkistan aus dem Nachlass von N. Th. Katanov*, Berlin 1933

MiklFremdSlav = Miklosich, F.: *Die Fremdwörter in den slavischen Sprachen*, Wien 1866

Miklosich, F.: *Etymologisches Wörterbuch der slavischen Sprachen*, Wien 1886

MiklTEl = Miklosich, F.: *Die türkischen Elemente in den südost- und osteuropäischen Sprachen*, Wien 1884–85

MiklTElN = Miklosich, F.: *Die türkischen Elemente in den südost- und osteuropäischen Sprachen. Nachträge*, Wien 1889–90

MK = Mahmud al-Kashgari's dictionary (after DTS)

Mladenov, S.: *Ètimologičeski i pravopisenъ rečnikъ na bъlgarskija knižovenъ ezikъ*, Sofija 1941

MSFOu = *Mémoires de la Société Finno-Ougrienne*, Helsinki

MT = Kahramanyol, M.: *Makedonyada'ki Türk ve Müslüman Toplumlarının Dilleri Konusunda Karşılaştırmalı Sözlük (Türkçe – Arnavutça – Boşnakça – Pomakça) (Üsküp – Kalkandelen – Gostivar – Ohri – Resne – İştip – Pirlepe – Ustrumca – Radoviş)*, Ankara 2002

Muchliński, A.: *Źródłosłownik wyrazów, które przeszły […] do naszej mowy z języków wschodnich […]*, Petersburg 1958

Nalivkinъ, V.D.: *Rukovodstvo kъ praktičeskomu izučeniju cartovskago jazyka*, Samarkandъ 1895

Németh, Gy.: Kumük és balkár szójegyzék. – *KSz* XII (1911/1912): 91–153

NEVP = Morgenstierne, G.: *A New Etymological Vocabulary of Pashto, compiled and ed. by J. Elfenbein / D.N. MacKenzie / N. Sims-Williams*, Wiesbaden 2003

Nikitin, V.V. / Kerbabaev, B.B.: *Narodnye i naučnye turkmenskie nazvanija rastenij*, Ašchabad 1962

Nikolъskij, N.B.: *Russko-čuvašskij slovarъ*, Kazanь 1909

Nowiński, M.: *Dzieje upraw i roślin uprawnych*, Warszawa 1970

OA = Demir, N.: *Ordu İli ve Yöresi Ağızları (İnceleme – Metinler – Sözlük)*, Ankara 2001

Omodaka, H. et al. (eds.): *Jidaibetsu kokugo daijiten. Jōdai hen*, Tōkyō 2000

Orel, V.: *Albanian Etymological Dictionary*, Leiden–Boston–Köln 1998

Özkan, N.: *Gagavuz Türkçesi Grameri*, Ankara 1996

Pekarskij, È.K.: *Slovarъ jakutskago jazyka*, Petrograd 1917–30

Pisowicz, A.: Weitere kurdische Wörter im türkeitürkischen Dialektmaterial. – *FO* 36 (2000): 235–45

Podolsky, B.: *A Greek Tatar-English Glossary*, Wiesbaden 1981

Pomorska, M.: On the Phonetical Adaptation of Some Russian Loanwords in Tuvinian. – *Zeszyty Naukowe UJ. Prace Językoznawcze* 117 (1995): 93–102

Pomorska, M.: *Middle Chulym Noun Formation* (= STC 9), Kraków 2004

Pröhle, W.: Karatschajisches Wörterverzeichnis. – *KSz* 10 (1909): 83–150

R = Radloff, V.V.: *Opyt slovarja tjurkskich narečij. Versuch eines Wörterbuches der Türk-Dialecte*, Sankt-Peterburgъ 1893–1911

RA = Günay, T.: *Rize İli Ağızları*, Ankara 2003

RAltS= Baskakov, N.A. (ed.): *Russko-altajskij slovarь*, Moskva 1964

Ramstedt, G.J.: *Einführung in die altaische Sprachwissenschaft*, Helsinki 1957

Raquette, G.: *English-Turki Dictionary Based on the Dialects of Kashgar and Yarkand*, Lund–Leipzig 1927

Räsänen, M.: *Die tschuwassischen Lehnwörter im Tscheremissischen* (= MSFOu 48), Helsinki 1920

Räsänen, M.: Der wolga-bolgarische Einfluss im Westen im Lichte der Wortgeschichte. – *FUF* 29 (1946): 190–201

Räsänen, M.: *Materialien zur Lautgeschichte der türkischen Sprachen*, Helsinki 1949

Räsänen, M.: *Materialy po istoričeskoj fonetike tjurkskich jazykov*, [trans. A.A. Juldašev], Moskva 1955

Rassadin, V.I.: *Fonetika i leksika tofalarskogo jazyka*, Ulan-Udè 1971

RAzS = Orudžov, E.H.: *Russko-azerbajdžanskij slovarь*, Azernešr 1955

RBškS = Karimova, G.R. / Dmitriev, N.K.: *Russko-baškirskij slovarь*, Moskva 1954

RChakS = Čankov, D.I. (ed.): *Russko-chakasskij slovarь*, Moskva 1961

RČuvS-A = Andreev, I.A. / Petrov, N.P.: *Russko-čuvašskij slovarь*, Moskva 1971

RČuvS-D = Dmitriev, N.K.: *Russko-čuvašskij slovarь*, Moskva 1951

RČuvS-E = Egorov, B.T.: *Russko-čuvašskij slovarь*, Čeboksary 1960

Redhouse, J.W.: *A Turkish and English Lexicon*, Constantinople 1921

Rejzek, J.: *Český etymologický slovník*, Voznice 2001

RJakS = Charitonov, L.N. / Ačanasьev, P.S.: *Russko-jakutskij slovarь*, Moskva 1968

RKirgS-Ju44 = Judachin, K.K.: *Russko-kirgizskij slovarь*, Moskva 1944

RKirgS-Ju57 = Judachin, K.K.: *Russko-kirgizskij slovarь*, Moskva 1957

RKirgS-O = Oruzbaeva, B.O. (ed.): *Russko-kirgizskij slovarь*, Frunze 1988

RKklpS-B = Baskakov, N.A. (ed.): *Russko-karakalpakskij slovarь*, Moskva 1967

RKklpS-BB = Baskakov, N.A. / Beknazarov, C.B.: *Russko-karakalpakskij slovarь*, Moskva 1947

RKklpS-ST = Safiev, T.S. / Turabaev, A.T.: *[Kratkij] russko-karakalpakskij slovarь*, Moskva 1962

RKmkS = Bammatov, Z.Z.: *Russko-kumykskij slovarь*, Moskva 1960

RKrčBlkS = Sujunčev, Ch.I. / Urusbaev, I.Ch.: *Russo-karačaevo-balkarskij slovarь*, Moskva 1965

RKzkS-46 = Sauranbaev, N. et al. (eds.): *Russko-kazachskij slovarь*, Almaty 1946

RKzkS-54 = Sauranbaev, N.: *Russko-kazakskij slovarь*, Moskva 1954

RNogS = Baskakov, N.A. (ed.): *Russko-nogajskij slovarь*, Moskva 1956

RO = *Rocznik Orientalistyczny*, Warszawa

Róna-Tas, A.: Altajskij i indoevropejskij (Zametki na poljach knigi T.V. Gamkrelidze i Vjač.Vs. Ivanova). – *VJa* 1990/1: 26–37

RTatS-D = Dmitriev, N.K. (ed.): *Rusča-tatarča süzlek*, Казань 1955–59

RTatS-G – Ganiev, F.A. (ed.): *Rusča-tatarča süzlek*, Moskva 1991

RTofS = Buraev, I.D. (ed.): *Tofalarsko-russkij, russko-tofalarskij slovarъ*, Irkutsk 1995

RTrkmS = Baskakov, N.A. / Chamzaev, M.Ja. (eds.): *Russko-turkmenskij slovarъ*, Moskva 1956

RTuwS = Palъmbach, A.A. (ed.): *Russko-tuvinskij slovarъ*, Moskva 1953

Rubinčik, Ju.A. (ed.): *Persidsko-russkij slovarъ*, Moskva 1970

RUjgS = Rachimov, T.R. (ed.): *Russko-ujgurskij slovarъ*, Moskva 1956

RUzbS-A = Abdurachmanov, R.: *Russko-uzbekskij slovarъ*, Moskva 1954

RUzbS-Š = Šanskij, N.M.: *Russko-uzbekskij tematičeskij slovarъ*, Taškent 1975

Ryumina-Sırkaşeva, L.T. / Kuçigaşeva, N.A.d: *Teleut ağzı sözlüğü*, [trans. from Russ.: Ş.H. Akalın / C. Turgunbayev], Kemerovo 1995

Scherner, B.: *Arabische und neupersische Lehnwörter im Tschuwaschischen*, Wiesbaden 1977

Schuster-Šewc, H.: *Historisch-etymologisches Wörterbuch der ober- und niedersorbischen Sprache*, Bautzen 1978–89

Schwarz, H.G.: *An Uyghur-English Dictionary*, Bellingham 1992

SEC = *Studia Etymologica Cracoviensia*, Kraków

Sędzik, W.: *Prasłowiańska terminologia rolnicza. Rośliny uprawne. Użytki rolne* (= Prace Slawistyczne 3), Ossolineum 1977

SEJP = Sławski, F.: *Słownik etymologiczny języka polskiego*, Kraków 1952–

Sevortjan, È.V.: *Ètimologičeskij slovarъ tjurkskich jazykov*, Moskva 1974–

Shaw, R.B.: *A Sketch of the Turki Language as Spoken in Eastern Turkistan (Kàshgar and Yarkand)*, part II: *Vocabulary, Turki-English* (= Extra Number to Part I of the Journal, Asiatic Society of Bengal), Calcutta 1880

SKE = Ramstedt, G.J.: *Studies in Korean Etymology*, Helsinki 1949–53

Skok, P.: *Etimologijski rječnik hrvatskoga ili srpskoga jezika*, Zagreb 1971–74

Slepcov, P.A.: *Russkie leksičeskie zaimstvovanija v jakutskom jazyke (dorevoljucionnyj period)*, Jakutsk 1964

Slepcov, P.A.: *Russkie leksičeskie zaimstvovanija v jakutskom jazyke (poslerevoljucionnyj period)*, Moskva 1975

Smolenskij, N.: *Polnyj karmannyj russko-sartovskij slovarъ*, Taškentъ 1912

Snoj, M.: *Slovenski etimološki slovar*, Ljubljana [1]1997, [2]2003

Spólnik, A.: *Nazwy polskich roślin do XVIII wieku*, Ossolineum 1990

Stachowski, M.: Khakas Food Names. – *FO* 31 (1995): 147–61

Stachowski, M.: Korean-Turkic Studies. – Brzezina, M. / Kurek, H. (eds.): *Collectanea linguistica in honorem Casimiri Polański*, Kraków 1999a: 231–41

Stachowski, M.: *Konsonantenadaptation russischer Lehnwörter im Dolganischen*, Kraków 1999b

Stachowski, M.: Notizen zur schorischen und tschulymischen Etymologie. – *SEC* 3 (1998): 107–23

Stachowski, St.: *Osmanlı Türkçesinde Yeni Farsça Alıntılar Sözlüğü. Wörterbuch der neupersischen Lehnwörter im Osmanisch-Türkischen*, İstanbul 1998

STC = *Studia Turcologica Cracoviensia*, Kraków

Steblin-Kamenskij, I.M.: *Očerki po istorii leksiki pamirskich jazykov. Nazvanija kulъturnych rastenij*, Moskva 1982

TA = Karahasanoğlu, Ö.H.: Trabzon Ağzı Sözlüğü. – *Trabzon Kültür Sanat Yıllığı* 87 (1987): 131–43

Tanievъ, S.-M.: *Samoučitelь tatarskago jazyka*, vol. III: *Russko-tatarskij slovarь*, Baku ʿ1909

Tatarincev, B.I.: *Ètimologičeskij slovarь tuvinskogo jazyka*, Novosibirsk 2000–

TDA = *Türk Dilleri Araştırmaları*, İstanbul

Tekin, T.: *Ana Türkçede Asli Uzun Ünlüler*, Ankara 1975

Tekin, T.: Türk Dillerinde Önseste y- Türemesi. – *TDA* 4 (1994): 51–66

Tenišev, È.R.: *Stroj saryg-jugurskogo jazyka*, Moskva 1976

TESz = Benkő, L. (ed.): *A magyar nyelv történeti-etimológiai szótára*, Budapest 1967–76

Tietze, A.: *Tarihi ve Etimolojik Türkiye Türkçesi Lugatı*, İstanbul–Wien 2002–

TMEN = Doerfer, G.: *Türkische und mongolische Elemente im Neupersischen*, Wiesbaden 1963–75

Tōdō, A.: *Gakken kanwa daijiten*, Tōkyō 2001

Tömür, H.: *Modern Uyghur Grammar (Morphology)*, [trans. A. Lee], İstanbul 2003

Tryjarski, E.: *Kultura ludów tureckich w świetle przekazu Mahmūda z Kaszgaru (XI w.)*, Warszawa 1993

Turner, R.L.: *A Comparative Dictionary of the Indo-Aryan Languages*, London 1966–69

TuwRS-Pa = Palьmbach, A.A.: *Tuvinsko-russkij slovarь*, Moskva 1955

TuwRS-Pu = Puncag, G.: *Tuvinsko-mongolьsko-russkij slovarь*, Ölgij 1986

UA = Gülsevin, G.: *Uşak İli Ağızları*, Ankara 2002

Ubrjatova, È.I.: *Opyt sravnitelьnogo izučenija fonetičeskich osobennostej jazyka naselenija nekotorych rajonov Jakutskoj SSR*, Moskva 1960

Urazmetov, H. / Bajšev, T.: *Terminologičeskij slovarь po botanike russko-baškirskij i baškirsko-russkij*, Ufa 1952

UzbRS = Borovkov, A.K. (ed): *Uzbeksko-russkij slovarь*, Moskva 1959

Vasmer, M.: *Ètimologičeskij slovarь russkogo jazyka*, Moskva 1986–87

VEWT = Räsänen, M.: *Versuch eines etymologischen Wörterbuchs der Türksprachen*, Helsinki 1969

VGAS = Poppe, N.: *Vergleichende Grammatik der altaischen Sprachen*, 1: *Vergleichende Lautlehre*, Wiesbaden 1960

VJa = *Voprosy Jazykoznanija*, Moskva

Voskresenskij, A.: *Russko-tatarskij slovarь*, Kazanь 1894

Wiesentahl, W.: *Dictionnaire de poche français-turc*, Constantinople 1895

Witczak, K.T.: *Indoeuropejskie nazwy zbóż*, Łódź 2003

Woodhouse, S.C.: *English-Greek Dictionary. A Vocabulary of the Attic Language*, London 1910

Zaatovъ, O.: *Polnyj russko-tatarskij slovarь (krymsko tatarskago narěčija)*, Simferopol 1906

Zaimov, J.: *Nazvanijata na carevicata v bъlgarski ezik. – Ezikovedski izsledvanija v čest na akademik Stefan Mladenov*, Sofija 1957: 113–26, 117–19

Zajączkowski, A.: *Sufiksy imienne i czasownikowe w języku zachodniokaraimskim*, Kraków 1932

ZDMG = *Zeitschrift der Deutschen Morgenländischen Gesellschaft*, Berlin

Zhen-hua, H. / Imart, G.: *Fu-yü girgïs: A Tentative Description of the Easternmost Turkic Language* (= Papers on Inner Asia, No. 8), Bloomington 1987

Druk i oprawa TERCJA s.c.
Kraków ul. Golikówka 77/1
tel.012-653-00-76